EMOTIONAL
Wholeness

The Healing Power of Love

CLINTON AGNEW

Copyright © 2021 by Clinton Agnew

All rights reserved. No part of this book may be used or reproduced by any means, graphic, electronic or mechanical, including photocopying, recording, taping or by any information storage retrieval system, without the written permission of the author, except in the case of brief quotations embodied in reviews.

Paperback ISBN 978-1-945169-62-5
eBook ISBN 978-1-945169-63-2

Published by
Orison Publishers, Inc.
PO Box 188, Grantham, PA 17027
www.OrisonPublishers.com

Unless otherwise identified, all Scripture quotations are taken from The Scriptures 2009, copyright© 1993 – 2015 by the Institute for Scripture Research (ISR). All rights reserved. Used with permission.

Scripture quotations marked as New International Version or NIV are taken from The Holy Bible, New International Version® NIV® Copyright © 1973, 1978, 1984, 2011 by Biblica, Inc.™ Used by permission. All rights reserved worldwide.

Acknowledgements

This book is dedicated to our Father, Yahweh, without whom this book would never have been possible. Your unfailing love has driven me to complete this work, after many years of contemplation.

I would like to thank my wife, Krina, who lovingly and not so lovingly, organized my writing, and spent many, many hours proof reading. To my coach Ron L. James who prayerfully coached me through the process, you helped me define a vision for the book and you provided insight to ensure that I made that vision a reality, thank you! Thank you also to the friends and families who encouraged me to finish the journey that I had set out on.

Lastly, the team at Orison Publishers, Inc. were also key partners, and I appreciate you for your investment into this finished product.

Contents

Introduction vii
Chapter One: Building a Firm Foundation 1
Chapter Two: Love Is the Cornerstone 19
Chapter Three: The Three Pillars of Self-Esteem 39
Chapter Four: From Broken to Whole 53
Chapter Five: The Helper 77
Chapter Six: The Purpose of Revelation 85
Chapter Seven: The Pain of Dealing 97
Chapter Eight: The Path of Healing 145
Chapter Nine: The Process of Wholeness 183
Chapter Ten: The Power of Action 197
Quick Guide 216

Introduction

Forewarning

I have spent many years contemplating the writing of this book and spent the last few months doing the actual writing. The journey has been incredible, and the path that I set out on when writing this book took a momentous turn right from the very beginning, for which I am most thankful.

This book was written initially as a pathway to emotional wholeness, but this thesis was quite flawed, for I soon realized that emotional wholeness is not the end result but merely a by-product of something deeper and more life-giving than what I was writing about. The essence of the book has now become the healing power of love.

We live in a world where symptomatic relief is sought after without any attempt to get to the source of the problem, yet it is in the source where the real brokenness is. We want to be set free, mostly from ourselves, but we are not willing to put in the effort to get the job done; thus, we often fail because we lack the desire to see the process through to the finish. This book will hopefully illuminate the way forward and what it will take to finish the job. I am by no means a world expert on any subject matter pertaining to psychology or the like and never profess to be one; I am a mere vessel, a shepherd boy, a Joshua, a Moses, one who has been called to do a thing for which I am not altogether qualified. So, my belief that I am being obedient and my desire to please Yahweh, my Elohim, are what have led me to this point.

This book is for all of us and is not intended to be a once-only read; you may need to come back to it many times and follow the process repeatedly. You will need to have the Word of Elohim at the ready, to review and learn and study these life-changing principles.

Before you start, there are a few things I want to share with you, to present you with a forewarning, if you will, about what lies ahead. This is not an easy-to-read book about how your life will radically change for the better if you follow three simple steps or how you will suddenly become whole if you say your prayers daily. No, this is a book that needs to, and should, challenge your thinking and shake the very foundation of your belief to its core. If that does not happen, then you are in great shape and this book was not intended for you. In that case, you should pass it on to someone who could use the help and should read it.

Firstly, I am a former professional soldier who served with the South African Special Forces, so the tone may come across as somewhat harsh; however, I assure you that I have a sincere and solemn desire to spread this message of love and hope in a very clear and unambiguous way. I want anyone who reads and grasps this message to have hope and a clearer understanding of the power of love. I am, by no means, the world's foremost expert in the psychology of the human brain; I do not have a PhD in any area, but I am a subject matter expert in this field. Furthermore, and most importantly, I am an obedient servant of Yahweh, my Elohim, and have written this book under His instruction and for His glory.

Secondly, any book can provide you with knowledge and skills, but only you, the reader, can change your own attitude and thinking. That is something you must do for yourself. The change has to be made so that you no longer conform to the patterns of this world but are "transformed by the renewing of your mind, so that you prove what is that good and well-pleasing and perfect desire of Elohim" (Romans 12:2). You will have to change your thinking and be transformed by the Word of Elohim so that you may prove it for yourself.

Thirdly, this book will not help you if you are not willing to "put in the hard yards." It would be like reading a book on bodybuilding and then not going to the gym. It will be of no use to you if you do not apply the acquired knowledge. This means that you will have to do the hard work in order to see the results; nothing will happen if you do nothing. You will reap what you sow. So, applying what you learn here will be a painful and hard road, much like that of physical fitness, but the more you do, the easier it will become. Be prepared for hard work and plenty of pain and sacrifice because you will receive your just reward in due course.

Lastly, and very importantly, the Spirit of Elohim needs to be your guide in this process. The Spirit has been appointed by Elohim to convict us, teach us, remind us, seal us, help us in our weaknesses, comfort us and lead us into all truth. This is my prayer for us in this, that the Spirit of Elohim be our guide so that we may see and experience the power of Yahweh, our Elohim.

May the love, the joy and the peace of Elohim be your portion.

Use of Scriptures
In this book I have used certain terms and names that I would like to clarify before we go on. This issue is important to me, so I want to make sure you understand why it is being used and why I believe it to be necessary in the book.

You will notice that I don't often use the term *God* or *Jesus* in the book; these are English terms used for our convenience so that we can understand the scriptures better. Think of it this way: suppose Giuseppe Verde comes to visit your church. He is from Italy, and when you introduce him to your audience, do you introduce him as Joseph Green or as Giuseppe Verde? I would say Giuseppe because that is his name, but when translated, it translates to Joseph Green. There is a difference between a translation and a transliteration, and I personally prefer the scriptural transliteration as it keeps the original words in the text. Therefore, you will never read any reference to God in my writing; I use the term *Yahweh* יהוה, which is the original Hebrew transliteration. I refer to Jesus in the book only as *Yeshua* יהושע, which means the One who Saves, for the very same reason, and the Spirit of Elohim or the Set-Apart Spirit when referring to the Holy Spirit. This is no sinister thing as I am merely quoting the scriptures as they are written in the transliteration I am using. Almost all scripture quotations used in the book are referenced from The Scriptures transliteration, and I have made every effort to quote it verbatim. I encourage you, when you read this book, to use your Bible to verify every scripture that I have included so that you can test every spirit according to the Word of Elohim.

All other terms and words used are explained or referenced in The Scriptures so that you can look them up yourself and allow the Spirit of Elohim to lead and guide you into all truth.

Shalom.

Chapter One
Building a Firm Foundation

The Beginning
It was 1999, the year that I got radically saved, both spiritually and from myself. I was not attending church, and I had just gotten divorced for the third time. My life was one big mess. My ten-year-old daughter invited me to a church meeting one Sunday, and I decided to go along. This meeting radically altered my life. The John Jacobs group, the Power Team, were "performing" at the church, and I can say that I was not impressed by their act. The Power Team was a group of strong men who performed feats of strength and then shared the gospel to those in attendance. As a former Special Forces soldier, I was not amused, to be blunt. Soldiering required that you put your life on the line for your country, and breaking free from handcuffs and blowing up hot water bottles till they burst did not exactly fall into that category, for me. But it was at that meeting that Yahweh found me when I was not wanting to be found. He had a meeting with me that evening, and it was there that my life changed. I dedicated my life to the service of Elohim and have not looked back since.

Soon after that encounter, I went to Mozambique on a mission trip to an orphanage, a trip that had a very profound impact on my life and taught me a very valuable lesson. On one particular day during this trip, we had a party for the children. Each child got a little something at this party—a balloon or a page from a coloring book, along with a crayon to color with—and when that was done, we handed out pieces of colored string to some children to make bracelets or necklaces. Each child got a little something, except one little boy who was about twelve years old. He got nothing because there was nothing more to give. I felt sorry for the lad, but there was nothing I could do because we had nothing left to give. So, when this little boy disappeared from the party, I was worried because I thought he was upset at not receiving anything. A short while later he reappeared with a needle and thread and started sewing up my sweatshirt, which had a long tear in it. I was in tears; this boy's action broke me because I wondered how an orphaned child, one who got nothing at the party, would be able to do something like this for me. It was one of the kindest, most selfless acts of love that I had ever seen or have seen since. This child, who had nothing and had received nothing, was able to find a needle and some thread to come and sew up my sweatshirt. This was the start of the road to wholeness for me; this one act of love compelled me to move in the right direction of healing. The lesson here, in case you missed it, is that we all have something to give, even when we have nothing but love. This little boy had nothing but love … and he gave more than anyone else did on that day.

A few weeks later, after returning from the trip, I was asked to go back with another group to the same orphanage. This second trip also had a profound impact on my life. I was counseled by some amazing people during that trip and my healing continued to grow and develop. I was invited to go to Canada for the summer of 2000 and had the privilege of attending the Toronto Airport Christian Fellowship, which was under the care of John and Carol Arnott. The interesting thing about this church is that it was the church where the modern-day outpouring of the Spirit of Elohim had taken place, and the church was buzzing with activity. There were three services a day, and people from around the globe were attending just to experience the outpouring of the Spirit. It was exciting to experience until I got to see the actual motivation of some people who were there. For example, one of the guest speakers was invited to "perform" at the church. The service was really good, and after every service people were invited to step up to the red line if they wanted an outpouring of the Spirit of Elohim on them. What really annoyed me about this was that a lot of people did not want anybody to pray for them except the guest speaker. It reminded me of fans rushing to touch their "idol." It was the most disturbing thing there that I witnessed. I soon realized that people were after the glitz and glamour of the whole experience rather than the experience of Elohim Himself. They were looking in all the wrong places. I had stood on that line many times and had not been touched by the Spirit of Elohim, and I was feeling dejected and sorry for myself until I received a very encouraging word from one of the ladies who was with us in Mozambique. The word was that I was looking for the wrong thing, that Elohim had more in store for me than this, and that I should focus on a relationship with Him and not seek for any outward manifestation. That word encouraged me greatly; I can gladly say that I never stood on that line again.

So, long story short, the experience at the church was an awesome time for me and helped tremendously in my growth, but two things from that time really impacted my life. Firstly, it was a time of healing for me personally. Things were revealed to me that I needed to deal with, which I did. Secondly, the church motto was "to walk in God's love and give it away." This really stirred me.

I came to realize that it is the love of Yahweh, my Elohim, that has the power to change and heal, and the more I delve into the Word of Elohim, the more I am convinced that this is true. My journey of healing and restoration has been and will continue to be based on the love of Elohim. This was the motivation that I needed for this change to happen. We need to understand the power of His love if we are to be healed and restored; nothing else does it for us. It was and is the only way to go from brokenness to wholeness, and this book is about that restorative, transformative and healing power of love—nothing more and nothing less.

The Journey
Where do we start then, with this journey of healing and restoration? The beginning is always a good place to start, but determining the beginning is probably the hardest part of all. So, when is the

beginning? Is it our birth date? Is it our first day of preschool? Or is it our wedding day?

Let us start by saying that there are two really important days in our lives: the day we are born and the day we find out why. Our birthdates are important because that date is the beginning of the rest of our lives on earth, without which we will never be able to participate in life and fulfill the calling that has been placed by Elohim on us. The day we find out why is when we receive meaning and direction to this birthday of ours, setting in motion the calling to which we were called and giving us the purpose of it all.

We need to understand how incredible our births were. We were formed inside our mother's womb, the winning sperm out of millions of others who made it to the egg—but I am not about to give you a lesson in biology or birthing because I am no medical professional. But, I do know that, biologically, each of us is a marvel of creation. Furthermore, think of this: at one point in the womb there were a million nerve endings growing from our eyes and another million nerve endings growing from our brains and, at some point, these nerve endings met and our eyes began to function. How awesome is that? Not to mention that we have sufficient DNA in our bodies that if it was joined together and stretched out, each of our DNAs would stretch to the moon and back—109,000 times.[1] Let that sink in for a moment. The only reason I am saying this is to illustrate that we are awesomely and wondrously made and have a purpose on earth, a calling that is unique to each one of us, one that we have been designed to fulfill. Does that mean that if we don't do it, it will never get done? No, not at all, but it does mean that we would have missed out on fulfilling our lifelong calling and died having missed out on a great opportunity to help others.

The second most important day is the day we realize what we are meant to do. This is an awesome day because, on this day, we receive a purpose and a calling for what could otherwise be a very mundane and unfulfilling life. This calling is not only for us, but also for serving

---

[1] "How long would your entire DNA stretch out?" *Answers.com*, December 13, 2010, https://www.answers.com/Q/How_long_would_your_entire_DNA_stretch_out.

others and helping them in their need. However, because life throws us a beating and stomps on us, we become broken and brokenhearted, have nothing to give, are empty and are in need of restoration ourselves before we can help others.

> *The value of a calling and purpose in life reminds me of Mother Teresa who served for decades in the slums of Calcutta, India, as a Catholic nun. She felt that it was her calling, her purpose, to serve the unwanted, the unloved and the uncared for, but this did not come easy. She had to petition the Pope for many years and request her release to be able to do this. At last she was granted permission and was finally able to fulfill her calling in Calcutta. This is an inspirational calling, given that she wanted to be in the slums caring for the poor and fought with the church until she was able to do so. This was quite something ... knowing her calling and then fighting to get to be able to do it. You and I should take heed.*

> *For me, that day came when I was thirteen years old. I had been toying with the idea of becoming either a game ranger or a flight engineer. One morning I woke up with such clarity as to my calling that I went to my mum and excitedly told her I had decided on a profession in life. Excited by the news, she enquired of me the choice that I had made. Beaming from ear to ear, I informed her that I wanted to be ... a professional soldier. That did not go down well with my mother, but I was not deterred and spent the rest of my life working towards that goal, much to the disapproval of my mother. Many years later, I resigned from the armed forces, having pursued my calling and having enjoyed every single day of it. Then I realized that there was nothing more to*

do—no more uniforms to put on, no more guns to shoot, no more planes to jump out of. Life had no meaning anymore, but, man, was I wrong. My years of service had prepared me for a very important stage of my life—a time of serving others and helping them to become all that they were designed to be. I had found out the true reason why I was born, and that gave me renewed vigor and purpose, without which we are lost.

Of course, these reasons for being are both factual, but life is what happens when we are making other plans. Sometimes it can throw us a curve ball, like a divorce, illness or death of a loved one that we were not expecting, and we are wounded, our dreams shattered, our lives destroyed, which leaves us broken and crumpled and in an untidy mess.

For example, consider this story about a top marathon runner who set out to win the world marathon championship at the end of the year. His whole focus was solely on this event. Forsaking everything else, he set about putting together the finest team of trainers, physicians, therapists, mental coaches and dieticians possible to achieve his goal for the year: to win the world championship.

The training was going well, the diet was perfect and everything he was doing was according to the plan that was put in place to achieve the end result. He was achieving his goals and accomplishing everything that needed to be accomplished. His mental health was the best it had ever been, his physical state was great, and his medical condition was near perfect. You see, this athlete had adopted a very intelligent approach to his year because everything he did was intelligent. From the coaching to the eating to the resting to the mental state, everything was meticulously planned and intelligently followed.

The year had gone by, his goals had been met, and his vision had been realized. The night before the race he had to go down the stairs to have his last cup of water with his vitamins, but on the way down he mis-stepped, twisted his ankle and tore some ligaments. The doctor did what he could and administered the correct medication while the physical therapist did what he could and strapped up the ankle. Everything that could have been done was done. Once again, his approach was very intelligent. All that being done, he went to bed and early the next morning he was on the start line, one of the favorites to win the championship. When the starting pistol went off, he bolted out of the gates and was in the lead pack for a while but had to abandon the race shortly after the start. You see, while he had approached the year very intelligently, doing all the physically intelligent things, he was unable to complete the race because he was not physically whole. His dreams were shattered by an unplanned event, something that he never foresaw, that took away his lifelong ambition and left him with nothing. The same is true for us in a way; we try and do things in an emotionally intelligent way, we approach things in a seemingly emotionally intelligent way, we seem to do the emotionally intelligent things when it comes to our lives, we try and apply emotionally intelligent systems to help us, but we fail sometimes because we overlooked one thing: we are emotionally broken because we are not spiritually whole.

> We are emotionally broken because
> we are not spiritually whole.

I wanted to share this analogy with you to illustrate that life does not always go according to plan and sometimes life is what happens when we are making other plans. We sometimes fail in different areas of our lives because we make terrible choices that negatively influence our lives and so become broken or because others make decisions that resulted in brokenness in us. From a position of brokenness, we continue to make decision after decision that lead to more brokenness, and we can never make a whole, undamaged decision as a result. When we are broken, we can only make broken decisions because brokenness breeds more brokenness. Only once we are spiritually and emotionally whole can we start to make more whole decisions.

We will analyze each component of this story so that we can fully understand the magnitude of this analogy. What did this athlete do that we could be doing, and what *should* we be doing with our lives in order to be whole?

Vision

The first thing this runner did was to have a vision, a clear-cut picture of what it was that he wanted to achieve, which is the first element. He needed vision; he needed something bigger than himself that would help him achieve something of greatness. This runner had a vision: he wanted to be the world champion. He set himself the goal and got busy planning the execution of it. Vision in the context of Proverbs is divine communication in the form of a dream or a prophecy or a revelation. So the thing we need is a revelation or a prophecy, some form of divine communication with us, so that we can become aware of what we are required to do. When we blindly go through life without this vision, we often wonder why we have landed where we have when we do. So, when we look at the word *vision* used in Proverbs, we find that it is the communication of the will of the Father expressed in our lives. Think about this phrase, "the will of the Father." It means it is His desire for us, His choice; so therefore, vision is a divine communication showing us the desire and the choice of the Father for us in our lives. As with the runner who had the desire to become the world champion, so it should be our desire to be complete and whole and to live the life that we are called to live.

The second element of vision is the intent. In other words, what is the intention of the person's vision? In military terms, the intent is described as a "concise expression of the purpose of the operation and the desired end-state that serves as the initial impetus for the planning process."[2] It also may include the commander's assessment of the adversary commander's intent and an evaluation of it. So, the intent is an important part of the process as it describes the concise purpose of the operation. Our adversary is the devil, and the Word of Elohim is very clear about our enemy's intention: it is "to steal, and to slaughter, and to destroy" (John 10:10). When we understand this and believe it,

---

2 *The Free Dictionary*, s.v. "commander's intent," accessed June 11, 2021, https://www.thefreedictionary.com/commander%27s+intent.

then we are able to clearly formulate our own vision and intent for the mission we are about to embark on.

> *As a young boy I knew I wanted to be a professional soldier and had decided that I would pursue this desire, if possible, until I had achieved the goal. I needed a picture of what it looked like, and, in my mind, I was able to formulate a picture of such a soldier. I watched some movies and tried to convince my mother to let me watch The World at War series on television, a request that was often refused. Not deterred, I read articles in magazines about the conflict in Beirut, and this really ramped up my desire to become a soldier. The idea in my head was to be the best soldier that ever lived and make a huge impact on the organizations that I served in. This did not go as I had hoped, due to many reasons, mostly of my own doing, but I did end up serving and had a colorful career. The two things I needed were desire, which I had plenty of, and an intent—a purpose and a plan that I developed and finally executed with success. Nothing starts without a vision. I needed a very clear picture of what I wanted, coupled to an immense desire and well-thought-out plan, so that the vision could be pursued.*

For now, we need a vision of wholeness, one based on the Word of Elohim and driven by love for Yahweh, so that we can live in the vision that He has predestined for us.

Motivation
We need motivation if we are to succeed in any task. We also need to believe that the attitude we adopt before we start any task will determine the success of that task. Motivation comes from two areas, inward and outward. People who have an external locus of control, or who, in other words, are extroverted, tend to be motivated by external

factors such as groups. They draw their inspiration from others, while people who have an internal locus of control, commonly known as introverted, are motivated by internal mechanisms. Their drive is within themselves. No one is one hundred percent one or the other and we are often driven differently at different times. So we draw our motivation from one of these two areas.

Our motivation is born out of a desire to achieve something, to attain something higher than ourselves, and we need that motivation to get it done. Without motivation we will fail because we will give up when things get difficult and painful. Our motivation has to be driven by love in order for it to be pure and steadfast, to finish its course and reach the end goal that has been set by us or for us. If it is driven by fear it will fail miserably, and the consequence will be disastrous on every level. We need to have a reason for why we need to be healed and why we need to be doing something in order to change. This is motivation.

> *I have seen this truth during my career in the military, especially when there is a selection process that takes place to weed out candidates. Candidates arrive with the dream of reaching the ultimate goal in their military careers, but these dreams are soon smashed to pieces because the going gets tough. During the first few weeks of the selection, it is largely group-orientated, so some candidates are able to feed off others and get the motivation to carry on. During the main selection week, though, there is very little group work and so candidates are required to find their own motivation from within. This is where the road ends for them because their locus of motivation is external, and when required to find it within, they fail miserably. Thus, when we need motivation, we need to understand where it is coming from and where it should be found when we lack it ourselves.*

Desire
Desire is a very important aspect because without it we *will* fail. Desire is the energy that drives us to excel, especially in the face of adversity. It is the primary and most powerful motivator we can ever have, and it should be fueled by love. Bear in mind that desire, when used in context of the Word of Elohim, has two different meanings. It can mean to long for or to ask for something, or it can mean a sexual or lustful desire—so it is important that we are able to distinguish between the two. In other words, if the desire brings about life and blessing, then it is godly; if the desire—immoral, sexual or lustful—brings about death and curses, then it is evil. Desire is a very powerful driver, one that is often underestimated. The marathon runner had the desire to achieve; it is what drove him daily to get up and pursue the goal set before him despite the pain and suffering that he, by himself, might have had to endure during the training. It was this desire that propelled him towards his goal, without wavering in his quest, to be the champion.

> *When I joined the Special Forces back in the 1980s, I knew it was going to be a tough year. The training was rigorous and long, and I knew there were going to be times when I would feel like quitting. There were a few things that got me through those times: God and desire. I would often quote scripture while walking in the dark and cold, lonely hours of the morning. And, just as the runner had done, I had set a goal for myself. I had a clear vision of what I wanted to achieve and so endured all the hardships to the end—because of my desire to become a Special Forces operator.*

Philippians 3:13-14 states this: "Brothers, I do not count myself to have laid hold of it yet, but only this: forgetting what is behind and reaching out for what lies ahead, I press on toward the goal for the prize of the high calling of Elohim in Messiah יהושע."

This scripture is clearly talking of the prize of the Father in heaven, but it illustrates the point that we need to forget what lies behind—not just put it behind us, but forget it—and then, straining forward, work hard to go on and press towards the prize. When we lack the desire, we give up too soon because of the pain and hardship; we fail to persevere and so rob ourselves and others of the opportunity to heal and to be made whole so that we can carry out the will of the Father who is in heaven.

Plan
Once the vision has been established and we have the enthusiasm and drive to get it done, we need a plan to execute. It is of no use to have this wonderful idea and all the enthusiasm but then not have a plan to execute it. The runner did; his schedule was laid out day to day, exercise for exercise and step by step. He followed that plan and, when necessary, revised it, but it was still a plan and it was still executed. Too often we have these great ideas about things we want to accomplish but don't have a plan to execute them. And when we do have a plan, we still fail because we have no desire and so fail to persevere. Planning also means we have a team of experts and specialists who help us achieve the goal we have set. We will never be able to accomplish great things on our own; we must realize the importance of a solid, experienced team when setting the plan in motion.

> *"Many are the plans in a man's heart, but it is the counsel of יהוה that stands" (Proverbs 19:21).*
>
> *"Without counsel, plans go wrong, but by great counsellors they are established" (Proverbs 15:22).*
>
> *"Commit your works to יהוה, and your plans shall be established" (Proverbs 16:3).*

We can clearly see that it is necessary to plan in order to achieve. The military philosophy is that when we fail to plan, we plan to fail. That is quite correct. Planning requires that we commit these things to Yahweh first, but we don't. We tend to want to go it alone because of reasons already mentioned; neither do we want to be held accountable for our actions. Planning also requires careful and prayerful thought and preparation, something which we also tend not to do.

We must plan in order to achieve.

---

*I am reminded of a story I heard about a woman who was battling with her weight and wanted to do something to start losing it. So she got hold of a diet plan, which was meticulous and well researched, and she got all the ingredients ready and was preparing to start the diet on a Monday (because we all know that diets start on this day). But she did one additional thing that was amazing and so powerful and very instrumental in her weight loss. She repented of her gluttony. She asked God to forgive her of her gluttony, and when she started the meal plan, she was able to lose weight and persevere because of her repentance. This woman had a plan, but she also committed her works to Yahweh—and **He** established the plan for her.*

In our desire to become whole and healed, we need to have a plan. We need to be thorough in our approach and believe that what we are setting out to do, we will accomplish. If we don't have this mind-set, then we are like the waves on the sea, tossed to and fro by the wind, and the Word of Elohim says that we are unstable in all our ways (see James 1:8).

Therefore, remember this: failing to plan is planning to fail.

Team
Once we have a plan, we need to put a team in place to help us achieve our plan because nothing great has ever been achieved by one person. We need to put together a team to help us achieve our dream. The

runner in our example had assembled the best team he could in order to become the world champion; he knew it was not possible to go it alone, even though he had the talent to get the job done.

> *Take, for example, Sir Edmund Hillary, the first man to conquer Mount Everest. What few people know is that he was not alone. When I ask people what the name of the Sherpa was who was with Hillary on the summit, very few people can answer. Hillary did not accomplish the quest on his own; he had a Sherpa, Tenzing Norgay, at his side. Even more so, he was part of a larger expedition that was led by a British colonel, John Hunt. Hillary was not even the expedition leader. But, on the day of the ascent, everything worked in his favor and he was able to summit the mount. However, he would not have been able to accomplish this feat if it was not for the rest of the team of which he was only a part.*

In order for us to achieve anything of greatness, it takes a team, and the bigger and more important the task, the bigger and more important the team should be. As the runner assembled the best team to help him achieve the desired outcome, so we should be putting together teams based on the size of the goal we want to achieve. Nothing of greatness is ever achieved by an individual, so our team has to be the best one we can assemble. It is for this reason that we need the Spirit of Elohim to be the team lead on the journey.

Execution
Once the team is assembled, we are to execute the plan we have made. The execution of the plan must be done with precision and confidence. It is well rehearsed and rehashed and every eventuality considered. There are many "what-if" scenarios built in and many plan Bs developed. Life is what happens when we are making other plans, and we are often unprepared for the things that happen to us because we had not rehearsed or prepared for them. Sometimes there are no plan Bs

Building a Firm Foundation

and we have to push through with plan A. I am reminded of a project I was working on one time. We were wrapping up the filming on the last day. The weather looked bad; it was going to rain, so the producer asked myself and my colleague what the plan B was in the event of bad weather. My esteemed colleague, without batting an eyelid, answered, "It is a wet plan A." It was an absolutely brilliant answer because sometimes there are no plan Bs, only wet plan As.

> *I remember going through a traumatic experience in my marriage, not knowing what was going on in the situation. It had been a long battle and I had taken a beating. I fasted and prayed and was given a book called How to Save Your Marriage Alone by Dr. Ed Wheat. I can remember only a few things from the book, as this was quite some time back, but the one thing that I can clearly remember is this statement: "Prepare for the worst, so that if it happens you are ready."[3] I am glad that I did, for the worst happened, and I was ready.*

The execution of a plan is critical to the success of the outcome because no matter how good the plan is, if it is poorly executed, the outcome will be a disaster. As for preparing for the worst, Mike Tyson summed it up well when he said that everyone has a plan until they get punched in the mouth.[4] To summarize, the execution is as follows:

1. The plan is well thought out and laid out in the sequence of events that need to occur at certain time frames;
2. The plan is the result of meticulous planning and preparation;
3. The plan contains the vision of the commander and his intent on the battlefield; and the plan contains a list of clearly defined tasks for everyone involved in the operation that includes coordinating instructions for everyone to follow.

---

3 Dr. Ed Wheat, *How to Save Your Marriage Alone* (Grand Rapids, Michigan: Zondervan, 1983).
4 Mike Beradino, "Mike Tyson explains one of his most famous quotes," *SunSentinel* (South Florida), November 9, 2012, https://www.sun-sentinel.com/sports/fl-xpm-2012-11-09-sfl-mike-tyson-explains-one-of-his-most-famous-quotes-20121109-story.html.

The execution of a plan is not a haphazard thing to be thrown together at the last minute and still expect the end result to be a massive success. We would do well to remember that failing to plan is planning to fail. I am a firm believer in the fact that the way we practice is the way we play. This means that whatever we do, if we do it often enough, it becomes the way we will do things in life. For example, if we are lazy during school, doing the minimum to get through the year, then we will become lazy adults and do the bare minimum to get through life. Remember, the enemy, the devil, also has a plan for our lives, and his plan is definitely not to help us live a fulfilling and enriching life. The enemy's plan is "to steal, and to slaughter, and to destroy," as John 10:10 says, and he has meticulous plans to ensure just that.

Self-Esteem
The final element of this analogy is the self-esteem of the runner. This is an important element, one which we all have in some measure, and it allowed the runner to hold a value and esteem of himself based on his capabilities and level of expertise. He believed in his abilities and his capabilities and was able to use that belief to achieve the goal he set for himself. We, too, have a self-esteem that may or may not be in great shape, but it is necessary to have a good esteem of self, if it is based on the correct things. The runner's esteem was based on his abilities as an athlete, and for good reason; he was accomplished in his field. For us, our esteem often takes a beating from the beginning of our lives. We are constantly bombarded with things that beat down our esteem. We need to restore our esteem of ourselves, but it has to be done according to the esteem Yahweh has for us, not man. Actually, we are responsible for the damage to our esteem as much as anyone else, and we need to have it restored to what it was intended to be. Having a healthy self-esteem is vital in the restoration process. (We will explore this issue in more detail later on.) We must not "be proud in mind, but go along with the lowly" (Romans 12:16). "Do not be wise in your own eyes," says Proverbs 3:7, which means that we are to have the esteem of Yahweh our Elohim—an esteem that will endure to the end and help us reach the goal set for us.

Building a Firm Foundation

There is a great story to be told about self-esteem in the film Cool Runnings where the coach, played by John Candy, is trying to get the Jamaican team to qualify for the winter Olympic games in bobsledding. The night before the qualifying heat, some of the team are in the bar having a few drinks while the driver of the sled is in his room going through every turn on the course. John Candy comes into the room and asks the driver if he is all right. As he is about to leave, the driver asks the coach why he cheated when he had already won two Gold medals. In the story, the coach had won two gold medals in two different heats but so badly wanted a third gold that he cheated in the event, except he got caught and was stripped of his medals. The coach responded and ended his answer with these words: "A gold medal is a wonderful thing, but if you are not enough without it, you'll never be enough with it." This is profound because we often seek out "gold medals" to make us feel better about ourselves—things like a great position or title at work, a great car or a big house in a flashy neighborhood. But if we are nothing without those things, we will be nothing with them.[5]

Summary

From the previous discussion we can clearly see that we need to have a clear vision with intent; we need a thorough, meticulous and well-thought-out plan; and we need a great team to help us achieve our goal. Once the team is assembled, the plan needs to be executed in order to achieve the desired outcome. All of these items need to be driven by desire, a desire so strong that it will propel us and compel us to persevere to the end. This desire is fueled by love, a love for Elohim only, not a love to be complete or a love to be comfortable—just

---

5 "Hotel room scene," *Cool Runnings*, directed by Jon Turteltaub (USA: Buena Vista Company, October 1993), DVD.

love in its purest, deepest and truest form. But even if we have love, we sometimes fail at achieving the goals we have set, not because we have not tried or not planned but because we are not whole enough, spiritually and emotionally. We try to accomplish things without being fully equipped, and when we fail, we become even more despondent and dejected, which leads to more problems. The cycle of failure needs to be broken, and we can break it if we are whole enough to do so. There is one key ingredient that needs to be addressed before we even get started, though, because it is the very cornerstone upon which this book was written. This cornerstone is love, the love of Yahweh our Elohim. It is written in scripture that Yahweh is love (see 1 John 4:8), and that is the very thing we need to go from brokenness to wholeness. If it were not for love, then our task would be pointless and futile because the very cornerstone of wholeness is love. The following chapter will explain and help us in understanding this love so that we may be armed and ready to go forward and become whole in Yeshua Messiah. Love has to be the driver of this process if it is to have every chance of succeeding. Love is the first stone of it all.

Chapter Two
Love Is the Cornerstone

Love

> *"For Elohim so loved the world that He gave His only brought-forth Son, so that everyone who believes in Him should not perish but possess everlasting life"* *(John 3:16).*

This is the start of the greatest love story ever to unfold in the history of mankind. The basis of the whole thing is love. We need to understand this clearly because Elohim's motivation was not pity, sorrow or anger, but love. We have yet to comprehend the power and the enormity of this love; when we do, we can live lives that are whole, fulfilling and pleasing to Elohim who created us in the first place. Back in Genesis, during the creation, Elohim decided that man should be created in His image to rule over the earth and the sky and everything that was on it. Elohim Himself decided that He needed earthly representation, in His own image, to rule the earth. This was not a "man idea"; Elohim created us, male and female. Why did Elohim do this? Surely He could have done a better job than any of us at ruling the earth, yet He chose us. He decided that *He* needed to create *us*, not the other way around. We know the story: Elohim created man and then saw that it was not good for man to be alone, so He created a helper for him, someone to be by his side. All was good until sin made its slithery appearance and the fall of man and woman happened. To put it into today's terms, we got infected with a virus because we clicked on an app(le) that we were not supposed to. Sin entered the world and continues to this day to take its toll throughout mankind. In biblical times, in order for the sins of the people to be atoned, the high priests would sacrifice animals once a year on the day of atonement. This practice was done so that the sins of the people were carried away by the sacrificial animals. The whole ritual was conducted by the high priest himself, in the holiest of holiest places. So, an animal, which was not to blame for the sins of the people, had to be killed so that those sins could be forgiven. This does not make any sense, if you think about it. Why did an innocent animal have to pay with its life instead of the guilty people with theirs?

The very creation that Elohim had made for Himself had been infected with sin and become something that Elohim had not intended it to be. Thus sin continued to abound and sacrifices continued to be made on behalf of the people by the priests. Elohim had a covenant with His people, which the people broke, so it had to be restored. Many articles have been written about the various covenants, which you can study, but I want to point out here that the covenant existed, which the people of Elohim broke, and like any covenant that is broken, it had to be restored somehow. In Jeremiah 31:31, Elohim declares that He has to make a new covenant with the house of Israel and the house of Judah. Why did He need to make a new covenant? The old one was no longer of value and had been broken by His people, and mankind's nature was sinful.

Baptism
Enter the Messiah, who was prophesied of in Daniel 9, born of a virgin, which in those days was a scandal of note because she was not a married woman. This virgin becomes pregnant and gives birth to this child who enters the world as a human and who lives and walks among the people. He lives a rather dull life until the age of thirty, when He is baptized by John the Baptist. This is an interesting event

for many reasons. First, John the Baptist is the only person who was born filled with the Spirit of Elohim, who received the Spirit while in his mother's womb. John gets to baptize the Messiah, which is an important milestone in the Messiah's life because that is when His ministry truly started. Jesus's baptism is an important part of the new covenant because it demonstrated to us the importance of baptism. It is symbolic of the death and resurrection of the Messiah who was to be crucified for us. The baptism in water is spoken of in the Word when Nicodemus comes to the Messiah and asks how it is possible to enter into the kingdom of heaven. Yeshua answers him, "Unless one is born of water and the Spirit, he is unable to enter into the reign of Elohim יהושע" (John 3:5). Here is clear instruction on baptism, repeated many times in the New Testament, because it symbolizes our being buried from the old life, being washed clean and being raised up into a new life in the Messiah. If the Messiah did it, then so will I. If it was good enough for Him, then it is definitely good enough for me.

Ministry of Yeshua
Yeshua continues His ministry for three years, performing great miracles and great teachings, delivering the oppressed and healing the sick, raising the dead and making the blind to see. There are a few stories in the Word that I would like to highlight because they serve to illustrate the underlying essence of these great miracles. The first one is where the Roman centurion comes to Yeshua and tells Him that his servant is ill and will die but that he knows Yeshua can heal him. It is interesting because the centurion, who commanded at least one hundred men, valued the life of the servant so much that he wanted him to be healed. Understand that the Romans were Gentiles and served pagan gods, but this man comes to Yeshua and asks Him to heal the servant. Yeshua agrees and tells the centurion that He will come to the house and pray for the servant, to which the centurion replies, "Master, I am not worthy that You should come under my roof. But only say a word, and my servant shall be healed. For I too am a man under authority, having soldiers under me. And I say to this one, 'Go,' and he goes, and to another, 'Come,' and he comes, and to my servant, 'Do this,' and he does it." Yeshua is amazed at this and replies, "Truly, I

say to you, not even in Yisra'el have I found such great belief [faith]" (Matthew 8:8-10). Here is the crux of this story: *faith*. You see, Yeshua is stopped by this man's belief, his faith. This unbeliever's faith moved Yeshua to act. We will see the importance of this in a short while. There are many stories of people acting in faith, which moved Yeshua to act and heal or deliver them. So, faith is a very important part in this whole picture, for without faith it is impossible to please Elohim (see Hebrews 11:6).

Death, Burial and Resurrection

Why is the death, burial and resurrection of the Messiah so important, and why is it relevant in the context of wholeness? We need to understand the importance of this event, an event so monumental that it has changed the course of mankind—an event without which you and I would never stand a chance or have a hope of living the fulfilled and whole life that we have been called to and predestined for.

Ephesians 1 spells it out very clearly for us:

> **"Even as He chose us in Him before the foundation of the world, that we should be set-apart and blameless before Him, in love, having previously ordained us to adoption as sons through יהושע Messiah to Himself, according to the good pleasure of His desire, to the praise of the esteem of His favour with which He favoured us in the Beloved" (Ephesians 1:4-6).**

So, Elohim chose us, mere mortals, to live "set-apart" and "blameless before Him, in love" (for Elohim so loved), having predestined, or already decided or determined, that we be adopted as His children by Yeshua. Why? Because it was, it is and it will be "according to the good pleasure of His desire." Elohim knew what He was doing and had already predetermined that the only way you and I could live the life He wanted for us was to be adopted through His Son Yeshua; there could be no other way. So now that we have the backdrop to the story, we can better understand the next story that is to be recounted.

Transfiguration

The next important part of the life of Yeshua is His transfiguration. This is where He is transformed before three of His disciples on the mount and is said to be the point where the Messiah becomes the connection between man and Elohim, much like the high priest was in the Old Testament. Yeshua was transfigured into the role He was sent to earth to fulfill and carried on His ministry before His death. The transfiguration is important here because it leads to the major event of His life. During this period, Yeshua is in Jerusalem and has the last supper with His disciples before His crucifixion. The supper is an incredible event because at it the new covenant, which Elohim spoke of in the book of Jeremiah, is revealed. Yeshua took the bread and broke it, and after blessing it, He gave it to the disciples, saying that they should eat it, for it was His body. Then, after taking the cup and giving thanks, Yeshua gave it to His disicples so that they all drank from it. He told them, "This is My blood, that of the renewed covenant, which is shed for many" (Mark 14:24). It is important that we understand that the blood is the representation of the new covenant that Elohim had made with us. Without it, the covenant would never have existed and we never would have been able to be adopted into the family of Elohim, as it was written in Ephesians 1.

Crucifixion

The next major milestone in the life of Yeshua is His crucifixion. After His transfiguration, He is prepared for death—the death on the cross, which resembles the offering of the lamb and the bull by the high priest in the Old Testament. You see, humankind had, and still is, fallen into sin. We had been "infected," and Elohim knew that the only way for redemption was to sacrifice the thing He held most dear to Him: His Son, His only Son in whom He had delighted (see Matthew 3:17). So here was the very sacrifice for us, for our sins and transgressions, for our healing and for our eternal salvation. This was the new covenant that Elohim had made with His people, that He would sacrifice His own Son for us so that we could live "set-apart and blameless before Him, in love," adopted as His children, because it was "the good pleasure of His desire."

You need to understand the enormity of this sacrifice. You need to comprehend the magnitude of the love Elohim has for us in that while we were yet sinners, Yeshua died for us. (See Romans 5:8.) This is not something you and I could ever deserve or work for. We could never attain the status of righteousness without this event, this life-changing event, but somehow we fail to remember, daily, how significant it was and still is. When we recount this event—and we should do so as often as we can—then we will not fail to grasp the magnitude of the love of Elohim.

> *I remember when I was freshly saved and was praying one day when I saw this picture in my mind so clearly that it has remained with me to this day. As I was praying, I felt as if I was falling down this dark hole, and there in the distance was a small light shining. As I approached the light, I could see Yeshua hanging on the cross, and it was as if my eyes were a camera and zoomed in on His bowed head. As the camera got closer, Yeshua lifted up His head and looked straight at the camera. I was expecting His face to be anguished and His eyes to be full of pain, but instead they were filled with this overwhelming love ... it was an amazing experience.*

His death on the cross was motivated by love for us, the unfailing love of Elohim, who sacrificed His only Son, so that we have access to a life in abundance. Now, I am not sure if you know what "a life in abundance" means, but I can picture what it is like. I can understand, to some extent, what it would be, but whatever it is, I would like to have it—and in abundance. I suggest that you watch Mel Gibson's movie *The Passion of the Christ*, released in 2004, for it depicts the life and death of the Messiah, and if that does not shake your foundations, then I am not sure what will.

The death of Yeshua is a very important landmark in the establishing of the new covenant that Elohim spoke of in the book of Jeremiah because it marks the end of one life and the beginning of a new one.

First Peter 2:24 says that "who Himself bore our sins in His body on the timber, so that we, having died to sins, might live unto righteousness – by whose stripes you were healed." The death on the cross was not only for the removal of our sins but also for removing every other weakness and disease that we could suffer. The Word of Elohim clearly differentiates between disease and infirmities, which means weaknesses, and these weaknesses are deemed to be any physical ailment other than sin or disease. It means that we are healed from any defect or disorder in our bodies caused by disabling or weakening spirits. So, His death is important in this context because it helps us understand what was accomplished for us on the cross. We have access to life, and life in abundance, because of this event. Our firm belief in this—our faith in the crucifixion, even though we have not witnessed it—will arrest Elohim and cause Him to heal us according to His Word. Without the crucifixion we would have no chance at a life of abundance.

Without the crucifixion there is no life of abundance.

We need to understand the graphic nature of the crucifixion in order to have any comprehension of the pain and suffering that Yeshua underwent for us. The movie *The Passion of the Christ* depicted it very well; it was gruesome and horrific and … words fail to describe the pain and anguish. Yet Yeshua willingly went to the cross for us, for our sins and our infirmities. Yeshua willingly paid the price for us because we, just like the servant in the biblical story who owed the master a fortune, would never have been able to repay the debt, no matter how much more time we had and no matter how much harder we worked (see Matthew 18). The debt was paid for us and the new covenant with us was established by Elohim through Yeshua.

This is another important lesson we need to learn here. We all are familiar with the death and resurrection of the Messiah, but we need to go back to it on a regular basis and remind ourselves of the fundamental importance of His death, His burial and His resurrection. We have to be able to grasp the absolute horror of His death. I think we have been taught the watered-down version of it; we have been shown the edited version of this marvellous event, accomplished for us by the Almighty Father because of His love for us. There is no pity here, no feeling of sorrow for us ... just the greatest love that has ever been shown to us as humans. We need to understand this story because in the context of this book we need to know and comprehend the power of the Almighty One, the power of His Son Yeshua, and the power of the Set-Apart Spirit (the Spirit of Elohim), so that we can be healed. If it were not for these events, then all of us would have had no chance, and I, for one, want to live the life in abundance that was promised to me and made possible by the death and resurrection of Yeshua Messiah, the Anointed One.

Resurrection
The next milestone is the resurrection of Yeshua. The resurrection is as important as the death in that it displays a few things to us. First, there is a way to conquer death, not a physical death because we are all going to die, but a spiritual death. We can be more than overcomers through the death and resurrection of Yeshua. His resurrection was the victory over death and hell and the conquering of the evil one that paved the way for us to follow to eternal life. The resurrection is a vital element of our faith and belief in Elohim, for without it Yeshua's sacrifice is but another story written in a book. His power over death in the resurrection gives us the hope of power over death, of power to live a complete and whole life to do the will of Elohim, according to His desire. The resurrection of Yeshua proves to us that the Word of Elohim is true and reliable; it proves that the forgiveness of sin is possible. Without the resurrection there could not be a new life. According to Romans 6:4, "We were therefore buried with Him through immersion into death, that as the Messiah was raised from the dead by the esteem of the Father, so also we should walk in newness of life." This is the importance of the resurrection summed up in one verse: the newness of life, the old things being gone and the new man arising. Notice the verse talks of the baptism or "immersion into death," yet again supporting the importance of the baptism.

The importance of the resurrection can be summed up in a few points according to the scriptures. First, it proves that the Messiah is the Son of Elohim; second, it proves that the Messiah conquered death; and third, it proves that the written Word is true. We have a living hope through His resurrection according to 1 Peter 1:3-4, where it is written, "According to His great compassion [He] has caused us to be born again to a living expectation through the resurrection of Yeshua Messiah from the dead, to an inheritance incorruptible and undefiled and unfading, having been kept in the heavens for you." Without the resurrection, you and I would have no hope of ever having a life in abundance. We would be lost and abandoned, left to our own devices and never having the chance of living in the desire of Elohim.

Ascension
After the resurrection, Yeshua ascends into heaven to be with His Father Elohim, where He sits on the right hand of the Almighty, interceding on our behalf (see Romans 8:34). Not only that, but Yeshua tells His disciples that He needs to go away because if He doesn't, then the Helper, the Spirit of Elohim, cannot be sent (see John 16:7). And it was important that the Helper be sent because the Spirit of Elohim is the power we need to face life and to live a godly life in Him. We are not left alone to our own devices; we are given everything we need for this life.

What is the importance of retelling the story of the death, burial and resurrection of Yeshua? How does the story fit into the context of being whole? Simply put, it is about faith. Without faith we have no chance. We need to believe that everything I've described happened and happened for us so that we may have life and have it in abundance. Telling it is about setting the stage for our healing and deliverance and getting ourselves prepared for the things that are to come. Faith is about the substance, the very reality or tangibility, of what we expect and proof or evidence of what has not yet been seen. (See Hebrews 11:1.) We need to expect to be made whole. We need to expect wholeness and restoration, and we need to believe it is there, even though we don't see it ... yet.

The greatest importance of this story is that, as a result of the death and resurrection of Yeshua, we are able to be saved. Being saved means we are no longer slaves to our old nature, but are new creations in Him who took the sins of the world upon Himself for us. This is critical truth to know and believe if we are to have any hope of restoration and healing, for it is the very foundation upon which our belief is built. Without this foundation we have no hope and no chance of ever being who we were destined to be in Yeshua Messiah, the Anointed One.

Character of Love

> *"To know the love of Messiah which surpasses knowledge, in order that you might be filled to all the completeness of Elohim" (Ephesians 3:19).*

    In this prayer, Paul is showing us the complete pathway of the love of Yeshua the Messiah. This passage describes how the Father gives us power through His Spirit so that we may "know the love of Messiah which surpasses knowledge," that we may "be filled to all the completeness of Elohim."
    In this passage, the writer is asking Elohim to rescue his life and save him for His kindness' sake. Other translations put kindness as unfailing love. This is an accurate phrase because the love of Elohim is unfailing; it says so in 1 Corinthians 13. So, why is it important that we deal with this concept of love? It is because you and I do not yet fully grasp the enormity of this love and the magnitude of its power and what it has done and can do for us. If we did fully grasp this love, His love for us and in us, then we would never battle with our own infirmities or struggle with our failings.
    We need to understand this love in the context of our wholeness, both spiritual and emotional. It is the underpinning of our healing, for without this love we are doomed. Why? It is because love is the driver and the power that sets us on the path to right standing with Elohim. It is love that compels us to change our lives, for we would not do it otherwise.
    Think of the story in Matthew 19 of the rich young ruler who approaches Yeshua and asks Him how he can get into heaven. What good thing could he do? Yeshua responds by telling him to sell all he has and give to the poor. The rich young man went away grieving, sad,

because he had many possessions. The young man was sad because of his love for his earthly possessions, and it drove him to walk away.

Love was his driver, but not his love for Elohim or Yeshua; rather, it was his love of worldly treasures. The Word of Elohim clearly states that where your treasure is, so too is your heart (see Matthew 6:21). When we are driven by the love of money, status or worldly things, then our hearts will be there, too. Love is a powerful fruit; it is the very element that drove Elohim to give His Son for us. We need to grasp this truth because if we are not driven by love for Elohim, then we will not be driven at all. King David himself was not driven by his love for Bathsheba; rather, he was driven by his natural lust for her. We need to have Elohim's kind of love if we are to be driven to Elohim.

Our motivation to get things done in life stems from either love or passion. I did a little digging in the Word of Elohim and found that every time the word *passion* was used, it was used in a sexual context. However, when the word *desire* was used, it could denote either a sexual desire or a desire as in the desire that Elohim has for us. That is why I detest it when people say that you need to "follow your passion"; that means you will be following the sinful, lustful nature of man instead of the righteous desire of Elohim. Our desire needs to be what gets us going, what starts us on this journey, and love is what needs to power us towards the end result.

> *"If I speak with the tongues of men and of messengers, but do not have love, I have become as sounding brass or a clanging cymbal. And if I have prophecy, and know all secrets and all knowledge, and I have all belief, so as to remove mountains, but do not have love, I am none at all" (1 Corinthians 13:1-2).*

This means that all we do is make a lot of noise, much like the proverb atrributed to Plato: "An empty vessel makes the loudest sound."[1] In other words, we are full of things, but empty of love. Love, at its purest, is the fruit of the Spirit of Elohim. That love is the most

---

[1] Plato, "Quotes," Goodreads, accessed May 22, 2021, https://www.goodreads.com/quotes/267603-an-empty-vessel-makes-the-loudest-sound-so-they-that.

powerful thing you and I can ever experience and have at our disposal to use and to live in and with. The love that you and I have on most occasions is weak and fickle by nature; it is driven by emotion and feelings that will fail us most of the time. Imagine if Elohim only loved us when He felt like it or when it suited Him. We would be doomed to death forever if that was so. Fortunately, the love of Elohim is steadfast; it is kind and unfailing and will never let us down.

So why is love so important in both the quest for healing and the quest for wholeness? To answer that we need to understand what love is, so let us look at what the Word of Elohim has to say on this matter.

First of all, the Word defines love as this:

> *"And this is the love, that we walk according to His commands. This is the command, that as you have heard from the beginning, you should walk in it" (2 John 1:6).*

The very essence of love is being obedient to His commands, and all of these commands can be found in the words of Elohim.

> *"'You shall love* יהוה *your Elohim with all your heart, and with all your being, and with all your mind. This is the first and great command" (Matthew 22:37-38).*

This passage contains a wealth of insight and knowledge into what love and obedience are. We need to understand this passage very clearly to comprehend the power of this love and how it needs to operate in our lives so that it can achieve the result it was intended to achieve. Being obedient to the words of Elohim means that we live in uprightness and respect towards Elohim and others. Love is not sin; it does not hurt anyone while sin always hurts others.

This truth is confirmed when the Word says this:

> *"Beloved ones, let us love one another, because love is of Elohim, and everyone who loves has been born of Elohim, and knows Elohim" (1 John 4:7).*

The next verse continues:

"The one who does not love does not know Elohim, for Elohim is love" (1 John 4:8).

We must understand what love is so that we can establish the character of love, and for that we need to look at 1 Corinthians 13. This scripture lists the characteristics that give love its meaning and its value, without which we would be severely lost.

Love is *patient*.
The Greek word used here is *makrothumeo*, which means not to lose heart, but to persevere patiently and bravely and to be patient with others who are not on the same level of maturity as we are.[2] We need to be able to persevere patiently and bravely and persist with this love. It is interesting to note that patience is a fruit of the Spirit of Elohim in Galatians 5:22, so the more filled with the Spirit of Elohim we are, the more of this patience we are able to exercise with others.

Love is *kind*.
The Greek word is *chrésteuomai*, which means to be mild, use kindness and to be kind.[3] Once again, this a fruit of the Spirit, which is no accident; because Elohim is love, His Spirit will also be love. We are to be kind to one another as commanded in Ephesians 4:32, "forgiving one another, as Elohim also forgave you in Messiah."

Love *does not envy*.
The Greek word *zéloó* describes it as the sound of boiling water, or in other words, to be boiling mad.[4] The use of the word means that you want to possess something that someone else has. This was clearly demonstrated by David when he stood on the roof of his palace and saw Bathsheba. He wanted her; he envied her; the word is often used

---

[2] *The KJV New Testament Greek Lexicon*, s.v. "makrothumeo," accessed June 11, 2021, https://www.biblestudytools.com/lexicons/greek/kjv/makrothumeo.html.
[3] *The KJV New Testament Greek Lexicon*, s.v. "chrésteuomai," accessed June 11, 2021, https://www.biblestudytools.com/lexicons/greek/kjv/chrésteuomai.html.
[4] *The KJV New Testament Greek Lexicon*, s.v., "zéloó," accessed June 11, 2021, https://www.biblestudytools.com/lexicons/greek/kjv/zéloó.html.

with a strong desire or commitment to have something or someone. Love, however, does not do this. It does not boil over, and it does not have the desire to possess other people's possessions. Your not coveting your neighbor's wife is a great example here.

Love *does not boast*.

The Greek word used here is *perpereuomai*, somebody who is a show-off.[5] It does not have pride in itself because this pride always comes before a fall. Love does not show off and does not need any attention.

Love is *not puffed up*.

The Greek word is *phusioó*, which means to be egotistical.[6] Puffed-up people are arrogant and self-centered and want all the attention for themselves. This word can be used negatively, too, when people seek attention for their afflictions or illnesses or circumstances. Love is humble by nature.

Love *does not behave indecently*.

The Greek word is *aschēmoneō*, which means to act in a manner not becoming of love.[7] For example, when you make inappropriate jokes about your wife at a dinner with friends, even though your words were intended as a joke, it is indecent behavior. It does not edify your wife and it is indecent. There are two trains of thought here: one connected to sexual indecency and one to moral indecency. Love does neither of the two; it is always morally decent and sexually appropriate.

Love *does not seek its own*.

Love is not about getting things for itself. It does not do things to fulfill itself and make itself feel better. It is not self-centered. Love is about doing things for others before doing things for yourself. Love is about laying down your life for your friends.

---

[5] *The KJV New Testament Greek Lexicon*, s.v., "perpereuomai," accessed June 11, 2021, https://www.biblestudytools.com/lexicons/greek/kjv/perpereuomai.html.
[6] *The KJV New Testament Greek Lexicon*, s.v., "phusioó," accessed June 11, 2021, https://www.biblestudytools.com/lexicons/greek/kjv/phusioó.html.
[7] *The KJV New Testament Greek Lexicon*, s.v., "aschēmoneō," accessed June 11, 2021, https://www.biblestudytools.com/lexicons/greek/kjv/aschēmoneō.html.

Love is *not provoked*.

It is not easy to anger and is not touchy. It is not quick-tempered or irritable. If it is, then something is terribly wrong and needs healing. It needs to be long-suffering.

Love *reckons not the evil*.

Love does not judge; it is not evil or destructive. It is not to be resentful, hold grudges or keep a record of wrongs when a fellow believer sincerely repents. The latter refers to a believer with another believer; in this situation, a mature Christian forgives and sees the purity of a fellow believer's heart instead of labelling him as evil and judging him according to his past mistakes. If someone is unrepentant or repents without the sincere intent to change, a mature Christian will discern that that individual is not a brother or sister in Christ and therefore will judge the person's behavior as sinful and see the evil in it. Other translations talk of love not keeping "a record" of wrongdoing. That reminds me of when my wife and I argue, and she brings up all of the things I have done wrong in the marriage in the past. She gets historical, not hysterical, as the phrase goes. Love does not do this.

Love *does not rejoice over the unrighteousness*.

Love does not please itself with the violation of Elohim's standards. In other words, love takes no delight in wrongdoing; it does not enjoy it when someone else fails. There is no gloating over someone else's mistakes.

Love *rejoices in the truth*.

Love rejoices in the Word of Elohim and in the power of it. There is only one truth, and that is the Word of Elohim. Love rejoices when the truth is triumphant.

Love *covers all*.

This means that love will protect or cover someone else. Love is a protector, not a destroyer. It means we will stand up and protect others when they cannot protect themselves. It does not mean that we will overlook sin and compromise because there is never a compromise. Love does not have sarcasm and does not belittle others; it protects them.

Love *believes all*.

Love wants to see the best in us; it looks past our weaknesses and failings. When we are sincere and are pursuing right standing with Elohim, love believes that we are doing the right things. It believes that we are reformed and born again; it believes that we are pursuing right standing with Elohim. It does not tolerate sin but believes the repentant heart.

Love *expects all*.

There is hope in love, an expectation for us to believe in others that they will do the best for us and for themselves, that they will not disappoint us and let us down. Love expects the best but is prepared for the worst.

Love *endures all*.

Love can persevere through tough trials and circumstances. Our tendency is to bail out when things get tough and find something easier because we don't want to deal with tough times. Love, however, provides us with the stamina we need to endure to the end. Love endures it all without bailing out.

Love *never fails*.

Love never fails. Our version of love fails, and I know that because I have done so on many occasions in my life. My version of love has bailed out many times and let others down. This version of love is not love; it is actually just our emotional connections and desires that we display to others and hope that they display them back to us so that we can feel good. When that exchange does not happen, we become disappointed and disillusioned and want to leave and find another source of emotional well-being. Real love, the love of Elohim, does not fail and does not bail. It remains steadfast and is the same yesterday, today and forevermore. Think about what would happen if

Elohim had to deal with us on an emotional level. What would happen if He were emotional in His love for us, just like we are with others? We would have no hope and no chance.

This unfailing love is what compelled Yeshua to go to the cross for us and die for our sins. He paid the price for our debt. Does that sound like something we do? Or do we want others to pay their fair share when it comes to debt? We want to hold others accountable for their portion of the debt while we ignore the debt that we are in. I am not saying that love overlooks everything because it does not, but we need to approach things in love and not in anger.

Unfailing love compelled Yeshua to go to the cross.

Love, then, at its purest and most powerful, is from the very nature of Elohim and is a fruit of the Spirit of Elohim. It has to be from the Spirit because that is where the power is. If love is not from Elohim, then it is not true love, and it will fail over and over again. True love is unfailing, compelling and powerful.

Hosea

The story of the prophet Hosea is a prime example of this love as described in 1 Corinthians 13. Hosea had married a prostitute by command of Yahweh. However, while married she is unfaithful and sees other men, a transgression punishable by death. Hosea, on the other hand, is faithful and obedient to Yahweh and continues the relationship with her. Finally Gomer, Hosea's wife, is taken as a slave to be sold, and Hosea goes to buy her back and restores her to his side as his bride and wife. His story demonstrates the love of Elohim in human form. We may think that we have it tough when we suffer some setback in our relationship with people we love. But here is a man who loves Elohim and is obedient to Him to the point of pain. When we love with the love of Elohim, then we are able to do as we are commanded and be obedient to His commands, even though it costs us and hurts a lot. This story is also a representation of what Elohim has to deal with every day with His people. We often act like prostitutes and run after our fleshly desires, but Elohim, who loves us unfailingly, has bought us back with the ultimate sacrifice that could have ever been made. Elohim sacrificed His Son so that we could be bought back. This action is quite substantial, and we should never forget it. Sadly, we do forget, and it causes us to wander off and lust after fleshly things instead of pursuing real, pure, unadulterated love.

Hosea chose to be obedient to Elohim in this command because Hosea knew that there would be a just reward for him, maybe not in his lifetime, but in heaven. Hosea loved Elohim and was willing to do what He said, and, in so doing, he showed us that love, as described in 1 Corinthians 13, is possible. When you read this story, you should be inspired to love, unfailingly. You should be inspired to be obedient and to believe that He, Elohim, will work all things "for good to those who love Elohim, to those who are called according to his purpose" (Romans 8:28).

The key here is choice. When Hosea was faced with the choice, he chose obedience over his own will. He chose to follow Elohim instead of his own earthly instincts. I am convinced that his earthly instincts would be to not marry a prostitute, and definitely not to go and buy her back when she left him and returned to her old ways. But Hosea chose obedience; he chose to trust in Elohim and His wisdom and do as he was commanded. The outcome is unclear, but this story is an earthly representation of the love Elohim has for us in that He chose us as His bride, even though we were prostitutes, and then bought us back from slavery, at huge cost, when we wandered off into our old ways. This story highlights every aspect of what love is, as defined in 1 Corinthians 13, from the fact that it is patient and kind, does not envy, all the way through to love never fails. This last one is the part that gets to me. Love *never fails*, yet we have on so many occasions failed in our relationships because what we have is not real love. Rather, what we have is some distorted version of an emotion, and when our emotions are put to the test, this love we have fails us.

I am summarizing Hosea's story quite a bit, but I want to point out what a compelling love story it is. It is a story of love, brokenness and pain; it is a story of obedience, perseverance and belief. For us, we probably would have ended the relationship in a heartbeat, moped around for a few weeks or months, and then moved on. Or we would have ended up living a life of self-destruction due to our brokenness, trying desperately to fill the void with other meaningless and shallow pleasures. But, love never fails. It is resilient and steadfast and perseveres; love "expects all, endures all" … love "never fails."

I have come to the realization that we have very little understanding of this love. We have read the stories and know about the crucifixion and Yeshua's pain and suffering, but do we really know the love that drove all of this?

> *I went to Toronto soon after I got saved and spent the summer attending the Toronto Airport Christian Fellowship. It was an amazing time of growth and learning and I saw, firsthand, a number of things that both excited and dismayed me. The exciting part was the love that I experienced during those ten weeks because the church vision, stated boldly, was evident: "To walk in God's love and give it away." The experience of the love of Elohim was so overwhelming it made me realize that the love that Elohim has for us is the key ingredient to everything.*

In Colossians 3:23 we are commanded that whatever we do, "do it heartily, as to the Master and not to men." This means that we serve the Almighty Elohim and not men and that everything we do should be in service of Elohim. But, having read a few verses back in this chapter, there is something else very important that is said:

> *"Therefore, as chosen ones of Elohim, set-apart and beloved, put on compassion, kindness, humbleness of mind, meekness, patience, bearing with one another, and forgiving each other if anyone has a complaint against another, indeed, as Messiah forgave you so also should you" (Colossians 3:12-13).*

This is quite a passage in that we are to put on, wear and live compassion and kindness and so on, as well as forgive as we have been forgiven. But, the next verse is quite a telling verse. It reads:

> ***"But above all these put on love, which is a bond of the perfection" (Colossians 3:14).***

Once again, love trumps all. We can have everything else that we can have; we can speak with all wisdom and power; and we can know all things; but if we don't have love, then we are nothing but noisy cymbals. We need to understand the importance and the power of love in our lives if we are going to be whole and upright. Love is the driver; it has to be. Everything else will fail, but love never fails. We have to get to the point of understanding that love is the most powerful motivator there is before we can even begin to live in it. We have to know that it is love that fuels our very actions or the lack of love that does not; there is no in-between and there are no levels of love.

Chapter Three
The Three Pillars of Self-Esteem

Self-Esteem

Think of your life for a moment and ask yourself two questions: What do you want to become? And more importantly, who do you want to become?

The first question should be easy to answer because it is easier to become something than to become someone.

So, why do we fail to become someone? I believe the answer is because we have not set a goal for ourselves in this area. Most people will have their careers mapped out quite nicely for themselves and will put a lot of effort into achieving these goals, but they tend to leave themselves behind in doing so. Very few people whom I have interacted with have set goals for themselves of becoming someone. They have developed their careers but not themselves. This tendency seems to be commonplace amongst us in that we develop our talents, but we don't develop our character.

We spend most of our time becoming efficient at what we do but spend very little or no time on becoming effective or better at being ourselves. Character does not happen, however; it is developed. Much like a tree, once it is planted, it will grow and develop, but it still must be tended to—it must be nurtured and pruned and watered and, in due season, it will produce good fruit. If the tree is left untended, it will still grow and produce fruit, but the quality of the fruit will be low and of little use to anyone. So it is with us. We, too, have to develop and tend to our character and prune it, which means getting rid of the dead branches that bear little or no good fruit. When we are left to our own desires, we will fall back into our natural default settings, which are sinful by nature, and we become what the ruler of this world wants for us.

You have to understand that the thief (the devil) only comes "to steal, and to slaughter, and to destroy" (John 10:10). He wants to steal from you at every turn; every chance he has, he will use to rob you of your joy, your health, your wealth and your desires, to name but a few. He, the devil, will also slaughter you, and I am not talking of only your spiritual slaughter, which is the most important, but I am talking also of your physical and emotional slaughter. It is not always the obvious things that are important. It is often the overlooked and subtle things that make the most difference.

There is a difference between topic and issue.

> *I am reminded of when I was unemployed, and my wife would put the washing in the machine and ask that I put them in the dryer when they were done. A simple enough task, but I often forgot because I got too busy playing golf or watching a movie, and when my wife would get home to this unfinished task, it was not good. After a few times I asked my wife why this was such a big thing to her, and her response helped me understand a whole lot more than I could have done on my own. She said that it made her feel undervalued and unappreciated when I did not do what she asked. You see, the topic was the washing, but the issue was how she perceived my lack of support.*

The devil wants us to focus on the topic while ignoring the issue, which is the dangerous thing to do. We like to do the symptomatic relief thing because it is easier—it requires very little effort and no real dedication on our part. Dealing with the issue is a whole different story because we have to be committed to the process and make real changes to ourselves, which is difficult and not easy to do. So, symptomatic relief makes us feel better for a while, but we have to repeat that relief and each time the dose of whatever we are taking has to be increased because our bodies adapt to what we are doing. The devil's aim is to kill us, spiritually, emotionally and physically, and he will do whatever and however it takes to accomplish his goal. One of the biggest issues we face as humans is the issue of self-esteem, and it is this issue that the devil likes to use continuously because if you have a low self-esteem, then he, the devil, has won most of the battle already.

We need to spend time on becoming better people. We need to be more effective, and for that we need to be better at being human. We need to be deliberate and intentional in our approach to this goal, as it will not happen without effort. The tree does not prune or nurture itself into being a great tree; it is tended to by the master gardener who is deliberate in his actions. Consider the gardener. He does not concern himself with the fruit that the tree will bear; he concerns himself with preparing the tree—tending to it and nurturing it so that it will bear good fruit in season. The gardener is more concerned about the quality of the fruit than the quantity. The reason the vines and trees are pruned is so that all the dead and useless branches are removed, thus improving the quality of the fruit. We should do as the gardener does; we should tend to our lives and allow ourselves to be pruned and trimmed of the unnecessary and dead branches that bear no valuable fruit so that, in season, we will bear the fruit that is valuable.

John 15:1-2 says it all when Yeshua tells His disciples that He is the true vine, Elohim is the gardener, every branch in Him that bears no fruit is taken away, but every branch that bears fruit is pruned so that it bears more fruit. Yeshua continues to say that the disciples must stay in Him because no branch is able to bear fruit on its own, and if the branch does not bear fruit, then it is cut off and thrown away and burnt. Then He states that if His followers—us—remain in Him and His words remain in us, then we shall ask for whatever we wish, and it shall be done for us. (See John 15:4-7.) Yeshua continues with this:

> *"As the Father has loved Me, I have also loved you. Stay in My love. If you guard My commands, you shall stay in My love, even as I have guarded My Father's commands and stay in His love" (John 15:9-10).*

Yeshua then adds this statement:

> *"These words I have spoken to you, so that My joy might be in you, and that your joy might be complete" (John 15:11).*

This is important because we note that Yeshua is once again referring to love and joy.

The Role of Self-Esteem

What is the role of self-esteem in our lives and how does it affect our day-to-day activities? This is an interesting topic, and I am by no means the world's foremost expert on the subject, but I will try and impart some biblical knowledge and wisdom here because I believe it is important for us to know and understand the role of self-esteem and how it affects our lives.

Self-esteem is defined by the world as the value that we, as individuals, place on ourselves; it is the attitude we have towards ourselves, either positive or negative. Now, this definition may have some notion of accuracy in it since we subscribe to this worldly view of self-esteem. For example, if we are overweight, it affects our self-esteem because we look terrible or feel terrible. In another example, if we are unable to do things well compared to others, then we have an inferior view of ourselves. But how accurate is this view?

Self-esteem is based on three pillars, with the first pillar being the sense of worth. What are we worth, not only to others, but also to ourselves? Is our worth based on what we can do to and for others or what we can do for ourselves? Gold has intrinsic worth, which means that it has an inherent and built-in value. For centuries people have sought gold because it has value. So, if gold has this inbred value, then why do you and I have to work to have the same value? Are we not more precious than gold to Yahweh? Did He not create us to be in relationship with Him because it was the "pleasure of His desire" (Ephesians 1:5)? We have come to think that our worth is based on our performance and on what we can do for others. We are taught that net worth is important, but we are never taught about self-worth. And, just to be clear, your net worth is not the same as self-worth. We have been conditioned to think that our worth is based on what we can do and not on who we are. Yahweh has based our worth on who we are, for if it was based on what we can do, then we all would be doomed to eternal hell. It is written in Romans 3:10 that there is no one who is righteous; we are not righteous in and of ourselves. This means that even if we were to be on our best behavior, that would not make us righteous. We are only made righteous through Him that saved us, so our worth is not based on what we can do; it is based on who we are. This worth is given from above, and we should fight hard to understand this truth.

You and I could never do anything to enter into heaven, but because Yahweh has given us our worth, He sent His only Son to die for us. Our worth is determined by Yahweh and Him alone, but we have allowed the world to corrupt us and our thinking into believing that we only have worth when we are able to do things for others. In other words, when we are able to perform well, we have worth. This is a lie. We must understand that our worth is based on the esteem of Yahweh our Elohim, not that of man. And, just for interest's sake, gold is refined at a very high temperature in order to get rid of any impurities. This temperature is between 1,000 and 1,200 degrees Celsius, or 1,800 to 2,200 degrees Fahrenheit. So, you and I, who are worth more than gold, need to be refined by the washing away of our impurities, so that the pure "gold" in us will be left. Sounds like fun, doesn't it?

The second pillar is a sense of belonging. Do we belong somewhere? And do we add value to where we belong? What is belonging based on? We all like to feel that we belong somewhere and that we are valued in that area. When we don't feel like we belong, our self-esteem is crushed because we feel inferior. I read a quote by John Maxwell once that said to the effect that "we are the most valuable in the area where we add the most value,"[1] and this is true for belonging as well. Often, we don't feel like we belong, but we add tremendous value to where are and so belong there. A healthy self-esteem will allow us to see it this way. Sometimes we fit in even though we don't belong there, but since it feels good and stokes our egos, we stay there anyway, to our own detriment. That is not a true sense of belonging. A true sense of belonging is that we know we belong there, despite the hardships and despite our feelings, because those trials strengthen us and prove our belief. Viktor Frankl, a holocaust survivor, once said, "If there is a meaning in life at all, then there must be a meaning in suffering."[2] Suffering is an ineradicable part of life, even as fate and death are. Without suffering and death, human life cannot be complete. This sense of belonging, as with the other pillars, is not based on feelings, but on truth, and that truth is the truth of the Word of Elohim and the power of His Spirit. Not every place where you fit is where you belong, and you will not always fit into every place where you do belong.

Not every place where you fit is where you belong.

The third pillar is a sense of competence. Are we competent at anything? If not, is our self-esteem terrible? *Competence* according to the world is what are we good at doing and how good we are at doing that very thing. When we apply for a job, we are asked what competencies we have for that job. If our competencies match the position and if we display suitable personality traits, then the chances are good that we will get the position. Our sense of competence in our

---

[1] John Maxwell, *The 17 Indisputable Laws of Teamwork* (Nashville, Tennessee: Nelson Publishers, 2001).
[2] Viktor E. Frankl, *Man's Search for Meaning,* Gift Edition (Boston, Massachusetts: Beacon Press, 2015), 56.

self-esteem should never be based on a skill set or a physical ability; it should be based on whether we are competent for life. And, according to the Word of Elohim, we are because it is written that "His Mighty-like power [the Spirit of Elohim] has given to us all we need for life and reverence, through the knowledge of Him who called us to esteem and uprightness" (2 Peter 1:3). Here we see clearly that we have everything we need for life through knowledge of Him, not through knowledge of the world or through great skills. Remember that I am talking about self-esteem here, so keep it in this context. We have been equipped for life through specific knowledge, but because we have conformed to the patterns of this world, we have allowed ourselves to be caught up in the lie that if we are not good at something, then we are useless.

Many people often mistake confidence for a sense of self-esteem because if we are confident, then surely we have a great self-esteem. This is not so because confidence is a by-product of competence. The more competent we become in something, the higher our confidence will be.

> *Think back to the day you first started driving. I am sure it was a little nerve-wracking because it was new and your confidence levels were not high. But as the skill level (competence) increased, so did the confidence, until it got to the point that there was very little cognitive thought process involved because the skill became so ingrained that you just did what was required to get the driving done.*

This pattern is true for every other skill that we master in life: the more competence we have, the more confident we will be. A lot of times in life we will be called to do something we are not good at, and our competence will be tested. This testing is necessary so that we can grow in areas that need growth. For example, Moses was called to lead the Israelites out of Egypt, but he was not equipped to lead the nation; he could hardly speak. But he was called to do a specific thing for Elohim, not man. This he did, and he did it well; he had many flaws, but he did it. You see, Elohim does not necessarily call the qualified, but He definitely qualifies the called, as Mark Batterson said.³ We have been equipped to be competent through the knowledge of Him, but we rely on our own skills so that we don't look bad when we cannot get things done. In these cases, we would do well to remind ourselves of Proverbs 3:5, which says that we must "trust in יהוה with all your heart, and lean not on your own understanding." That means everything, not just the stuff we think is right or good, but everything. Our competence must be based in Yahweh alone, not in our own abilities. That does not mean we are not gifted to do things, and to do them well, because we are gifted in one way or another. However, each gift we are given is to be used to glorify the very One who has gifted it to us as well as to build up others; it is not for our own glory or edification.

> *As for me personally, I was called to ministry with juvenile delinquents in early 2000, and I felt that I was not qualified to do the calling. I had served for almost three decades as a professional soldier, and working with delinquent teenagers was not my thing at all. However, I was obedient to the calling and spent several years doing the work that I was called to do. Interestingly enough, all my years of military service had prepared me for this calling. I trusted in my own judgment at first but realized that Elohim had much bigger and better ideas than I did, as He always does. I dealt with just about everything I could think of and was always prepared for the task at hand, not because of me, but because of His divine wisdom in me. I had been prepared for this calling from an early age, and everything I had been taught in the military was what I needed in this ministry.*
>
> **"Trust in יהוה with all your heart, and lean not on your own understanding" (Proverbs 3:5).**

---

3 Mark Batterson, *The Circle Maker* (Grand Rapids, Michigan: Zondervan, 2011).

Our competence, our value and our worth are based on the functioning of the Spirit of Elohim in us. We need to be very wary of pride in our lives because pride has a way of letting us think we know better than Elohim. When that happens, we are doomed to fall because, as Proverbs 16:18 says, pride goes before destruction and a haughty (arrogant) spirit before a fall.

We need to have our self-esteem based on what the Word of Elohim has to say on this matter. Firstly, self-esteem is the esteem we have of our self, not based on human understanding, but based on the truth of the Word of Elohim. Psalm 139 is a great starting point, as it establishes the awesomeness of Yahweh in our lives. Hear what I am saying: it establishes the awesomeness of *Yahweh*, not of ourselves. When we read this psalm in its entirety, we realize who we are in Elohim, not in ourselves. We come to understand that we have a value far above that which we can ever give to ourselves or achieve on our own. We come to know who we are in Him, the very One who created us in His image. Let us have a look at what the Word of Elohim has to say about us in Psalm 139.

The first verse states that Yahweh has searched us and known us. It says that we have been searched by the Almighty, Creator of heaven and earth. Now, why would the Almighty Elohim have searched us and known us? How are we this important, that we are known by the very One who created us? We are important to Elohim because we were created to be in relationship with Him. But, because we sinned, we separated ourselves from Him and allowed the devil to infect us with a virus that has distorted our view of self ever since. In the sixth verse of the psalm, the psalmist states that this knowledge is too wondrous for him; it is high, and he is unable to reach it. So, the knowledge that Yahweh has of us is so wondrous and so high that we will not be able to reach it or understand it. It seems like we have some value and worth, if this is the case! In verse 14 the writer declares his thanks to Elohim, for he is awesomely and wondrously made. This statement is awesome, for when we understand that Elohim made us awesomely and wondrously, then we will begin to understand our worth and value.

> *Remember how your eyes were created? When you were being awesomely and wondrously made, a million nerve endings grew from the brain to the eyeball, and a million nerve endings grew from the eye to the brain. At some point these endings connected to one another, and you had sight.*

In verse 16, the writer states that Elohim saw his unformed body, meaning that while he was being formed, Elohim was looking at him. I have always imagined that when sight is established in the womb and the unborn baby opens its eyes for the first time, the first thing it sees is Elohim. I can just picture that happening. Also, our human DNA is quite amazing. Remember, if it were attached to one another and stretched out, it would extend to the moon and back almost 109,000 times.[4] Now, I don't know about you, but this is quite an amazing bit of engineering created by a loving, just and merciful Creator who has awesomely and wondrously made us. If this knowledge does not help to convince you that you have value and worth, then I am not sure what will. We have been awesomely and wondrously made—I am convinced of it—and I am convinced that my value and worth has been decided for me already by the very Creator who put me on this earth. The sum here gets quite spectacular when you start doing some math.

> *Think of this: in the race of sperm cells to impregnate an egg, there are between 15 and 259 **million** sperm cells per milliliter, and between 1.5 and 7.5 milliliters of fluid expelled, and out of all of these sperm cells, you and I were the winner. I know it might seem a bit graphic, but it is so awesome that it is worth talking about. We are talking of millions of sperm here, but you and I were chosen to be the one. If this is the case—which it is—then you and I have worth and we have value. Take this one step*

---

[4] "How long would your entire DNA stretch out?" *Answers.com*, December 13, 2010

further, and consider that in the act of sex, we have been given the authority, by Yahweh, to procreate, which means to create on behalf of and populate the earth. This is a huge deal, one that I think we have taken for granted, since we have become dulled in our senses as to how great this responsibility is. We, then, must have worth and value if Elohim has given us this authority and purpose in life.

In verse 15, the writer declares that he was "shaped in a hidden place, knit together in the depths of the earth." Here the knitting together is a great metaphor for how our bodies are put together.

It is like our grandmothers who knit a pullover or jersey. It requires some careful thought and consideration as to what is to be made, what color it is, how much wool will be required to get the job done, and what size needles will be used. All of this is done according to a pattern. Different types of stitches are used to highlight certain areas of the garment. When the garment is finished, there is a wonderful product that has been lovingly made by a skilled craftsman. Psalm 139 tells me the same story: there is a pattern that is used, although no two garments are alike. Each one of us has an identification code in our DNA, and each of us has unique fingerprints not repeated by anyone else. We are awesomely and wondrously made, I tell you.

Further on in Psalm 139 the writer states that the thoughts of Elohim to him are more than the grains of sand, which begs the question as to why Elohim would think of us this much if we had no value and no worth. The psalm ends with the writer asking Elohim to search him again, to try him and to know his thoughts. The purpose was so that any idolatrous way could be identified in the writer and he could be led by Elohim in the way everlasting.

This psalm stirs me up and helps me realize how awesomely and wondrously we are made. It helps me to realize that we are worth more than diamonds and gold and that we have a value so great that only the death, the sacrifice, of the only Son of Yahweh would be enough to redeem us and let us live a life of abundance for Him. Yet, we allow things in life to overtake us and destroy us. We allow the lies of the devil to fool us and trick us into thinking that we have no value and worth and that we will never be good enough. This is true for many people because they fall for those lies and do things that undermine their value and worth, things that hurt or destroy them.

> Our value is so great that only the death
> of the Son of Yahweh could redeem us.

When we fall for the lies of the devil, then he, the devil, gets us to do the dirty work that he has set out to do. For example, if our weak point is the love of money, then the devil will ensure that we have a lot of it; that way we don't have to rely on anything or anyone else. The Word of Elohim says that the love of money is the root of all evil (see 1 Timothy 6:10)—is it any wonder that a lot of people who lose all of their worldly wealth then turn to Yahweh for help? If addiction is our problem, then the devil will keep us addicted so that he does not have to worry about us being set free. When our esteem is based on external things, we will forever be caught up in the downward spiral of death and destruction and seek external things to keep our esteem boosted. But when our esteem is based on Yahweh, our Elohim, then we will live a life in abundance and freedom and victory because we will have the Spirit of Elohim who gives us our esteem. We will not have need of anything externally to help us in this area. The devil knows this and will do anything in his power to stop us from having a spiritually healthy esteem based in Elohim. Then he can execute his plan of stealing, slaughtering and destroying as stated in John 10:10.

This has been the devil's strategy since the beginning, when he attacked us on the level of our esteem. He has not stopped since. Eve, in the Garden of Eden, was attacked through her esteem. Think about this for minute: the serpent entices Eve by saying that if she ate of the fruit, then she would be as knowledgeable as Yahweh. The devil tempted her in the area of her esteem because if her esteem was good, then she would have had no problem in resisting the temptation. However, because her esteem of herself was vulnerable, she succumbed to the sin, and we know the rest of the story. When we have a healthy esteem of self, based in Elohim, then we are able to function as we ought, and we will be able to withstand the schemes of the devil.

We need to develop and nurture a sense of self-esteem in ourselves and in others. In order to do this, we need to understand the role of a healthy, sound esteem, have a healthy self-esteem and continually develop our self-esteem based on the Word of Elohim (not of ourselves or of men). Be diligent in these three admonitions. Be responsible and "be sober, watch, because your adversary the devil walks about like a roaring lion, seeking someone to devour" (1 Peter 5:8). The next verse continues, "Resist him, firm in the belief, knowing that the same hardships are experienced by your brotherhood in the world" (1 Peter 5:9). Then the passage ends with this:

> **"And the Elohim of all favour, who called you to His everlasting esteem by Messiah Yeshua, after you have suffered a while, Himself perfect, establish, strengthen, and settle you. To Him be the esteem and the might forever and ever. Amen" (1 Peter 5:10-11).**

Chapter Four
From Brokenness to Wholeness

Road Trip
The journey from brokenness to wholeness is like a road trip, a great adventure, filled with many sights and opportunities and wonderful places to be explored. But the reality is that it also can be a time of many dangers and detours and difficult places that we are unaware of. Nevertheless, in order to get from where we are to where we want to be, we have to go on this trip. And when we do go, if we go, we will need to do some planning. It is great to sometimes just get up and go without much planning, which in itself is quite an adventure. When we are planning this journey from brokenness to wholeness, though, we cannot leave things to chance. We cannot just go on a whim and hope for the best. The trip needs to be prayerfully considered and our works submitted to Yahweh, who will establish our plans (see Proverbs 16:3). Thus there are a few key elements to this trip that we must explore and understand before leaving so that we have every chance of success and of reaching where we need to be.

Desire
Desire is fueled by love—the love for what we do. If it was not fueled by love, then we leave or abandon the thing we are doing and find

another thing to keep us busy. Jobs, relationships, marriages—all fall under this hammer. When we don't like the thing we are doing or the relationship we are in because we have "fallen out of love" with it, then we move on and find the next thing to love. This, then, is not real love. It is only affection and the immediate emotional stimulus we long for that keeps us there. Once this emotional stimulus is done, so are we. Love, on the other hand, does not disappoint us and does not fail us. Rather, it drives us to persevere until the job is done or the race is finished. Remember 1 Corinthians 13: love covers all, believes all, expects all, endures all … love never fails.

The price for success is also sometimes high, and oftentimes we are not willing to sacrifice some things in order to achieve others. If our desire is to be healthy but we fail to sacrifice our bad eating habits, then we will not achieve our goal. We failed to make the necessary sacrifices in order to achieve the goal. We can read all the best books on healthy eating and healthy living, but if we don't sacrifice our unhealthy habits and actively pursue healthy ones, then we will achieve nothing but failure. This failure comes with a price, too. Once we fail, we will see ourselves as failures and we will begin to think that we are not capable of winning. This train of thought takes hold in our life, and eventually we begin to live our thoughts. "For as he reckons [estimates] in his life, so is he" (Proverbs 23:7).

Now, there is nothing wrong with failing when you are actively pursuing a goal. For example, when you are working on your marriage to be a more effective partner and you do not get it right, then you have failed, but you have failed forward. In other words, you simply have not succeeded in your attempts to improve. If, on the other hand, you should be working on your marriage and are not, then you have failed backwards, simply because you have not even attempted to be more effective.

Belief without works is dead. We need to act on what we say and on what we believe. Belief is not what we say. It is when we do what we say. Desire is therefore needed if we are to go from brokenness to wholeness; we need to have the desire to be whole and complete and lacking in nothing (see James 1:4). Without this desire, we will fail.

Aim

After desire, there has to be an aim. There needs to be something that must be achieved. Without goals, we wander aimlessly, hoping to achieve something that we have never decided on. Think of it this way. When we are firing a gun or shooting an arrow, we are trying to aim it in a certain direction to hit some target or to achieve something by doing so. It is not a pointless act. We have to aim the weapon at the target in order to hit the mark. The aim is the very thing that directs us to go in a certain direction. It sets us up for movement.

> *When planning military operations, the very first step is to determine the aim of the operation because, when this is done, the rest of the planning is tested against the aim. So, if the aim is to neutralize the enemy, then all of the planning is geared towards neutralizing them. There is no deviation because if there is, the aim of the mission is not achieved.*

So, the aim is paramount. It is the first step in your journey to wholeness; you need to decide what the aim is. Think of your life, your marriage or your career and ask if what you are doing is the right direction for you to be going in. If you have trouble deciding what the aim is, then I suggest you read Psalm 139 in its entirety. You need to know the aim given by Elohim for your life because the psalm says that He, Elohim, has written every day of your life before you were even thought of (see verse 16). Get the aim in place, for this will shape the direction in which you are traveling. The aim is the starting point of going in the right direction. Determine the aim of your life. It should be to live "set-apart and blameless before Him," who chose us in love (Ephesians 1:4). Write this aim down and look at it often; memorize it and quote it often. Everything you do should align with your aim. If it does not, then you are doing the wrong things. This aim directs you daily to do the things that will help you achieve your goal.

Goals

Determine goals for yourself. These are interim goals that you can achieve while on your way to the end result. For example, if you set a goal of losing fifteen pounds, then the first few goals are to change your eating habits, start exercising and begin getting active. This does not mean that you go from zero to three hours of exercise every day. Rather, it means that you make small changes at first because, as you make these changes and you see results, you are driven even more to carry on.

We often set ourselves up for failure in that we set these lofty goals, which are not necessarily bad, but are big and out of reach. Then, when we don't hit the mark, we become discouraged and give up altogether. The Word says that "expectancy drawn out makes the heart sick, but a longing come true is a tree of life" (Proverbs 13:12). In other words, when we expect something that is not going to happen or that will take a long time to come to fruition, then we become discouraged and resentful. When the longing is fulfilled, though, it gives us life. When we set goals that we can never achieve, or when we never plan properly to achieve these goals, we give up when we fail. We set ourselves up for failure. This is what happens for most things in our lives. We have this expectancy for things to be a certain way, but when those expectations are not met, we become despondent, resentful, hurt and broken. We are responsible for most of this failure because we never set goals for ourselves and have no aim. With no aim, we will fail to hit the mark time after time.

Belief without action is useless.

Setting goals is an important step in this process—specifically goals that are in alignment with your aim. For example, if your aim is to be healthy, then your goal should be to exercise more and eat well. You should not become despondent at not achieving your desire if you eat unhealthy foods and fail to exercise. Belief without action is useless. But, once again, when these goals are fueled by a desire to be well, to be healthy, then achieving them becomes easier. Here is a simple test: whatever you are doing the most of, that is where your desire is. Whatever you are obedient to is your master. (See Romans 6:16.) Setting goals is important because it allows you to track your progress on the journey towards the aim.

> *I remember going on one of these trips when I retired from the military. I had bought a Harley motorcycle and decided that a road trip was the thing to do. So, a friend and I decided to meet up on a Sunday at noon at a rendezvous and travel to another big city where he could have his motorcycle serviced the next day. That was the sum of our planning for a two-week epic adventure. But it was epic. Every day we would take out a road map and look at it to decide where we wanted to be by the end of the day. Then we headed out following whatever route was the most scenic. We would arrive at our destination, set up camp, and repeat—daily.*

Destination
Where are you going? Where is your life path headed for? Are you on the path that you wanted to be on, or are you on some unfamiliar and uncharted route that you never intended to be on?

We often set out on a path in life hoping that we will land up somewhere good. Instead we land somewhere completely different. It is a simple principle: the path you are on will take you to where the path leads and not necessarily to where you want to be. It makes sense, doesn't it? When you get on a road that leads to a major city, then you will eventually get to that major city. You cannot get anywhere else unless you take another route. Life is like this for us. We start out on a route to reach a destination of our choosing, but then we take some detours in life and end up somewhere else, much to our disappointment. But we should not be disappointed; we are the ones who made a series of choices that led us there. For example, we cannot be disappointed when we are unhealthy and our medical bills spiral out of control. We are the ones who made poor lifestyle choices for most of our lives. The world is not against you; you are mostly against yourself. There are times when life will throw us a curveball or two, but we still have the ability to make choices.

> *There is an amazing quote by Viktor Frankl, a Holocaust survivor. He said, "Everything can be taken from a man but one thing: the last of the human freedoms—to choose one's attitude in any given set of circumstances, to choose one's own way."[1]*

Even when life throws these curveballs at us, we still have the power of choice. This is the only right we really have, given to us by Elohim, and we need to exercise this right daily. We can choose where we are headed in life, even though we may take some detours along the way. It might take us just a little longer to reach the destination that we have set, but we can still get there. We only fail when we stop trying. We need to have an aim for everything we want to achieve, otherwise we will land up somewhere else and become disillusioned with ourselves, with others and with life.

If you don't have an end goal in mind, you can land up anywhere. Then it won't matter where you are because you have planned to be nowhere. But when you plan this trip and set a goal and an end state for yourself and pursue it, then you will get to where you want to be. But you have to be intentional—that means to have purpose—and be deliberate in your approach. You have to be meticulous with your plans and then pursue making it happen. When you fail to plan, you plan to fail.

Here I am reminded again of belief, of faith in Elohim who had commanded Abraham to pack up and leave. He commanded Abram to "go yourself out of your land, from your relatives and from your father's house, to a land which I show you" (Genesis 12:1). Here is a great example of belief in action. For Abram to pack up and go was not a simple task; it required some planning and preparation. But, here

---

1 Viktor E. Frankl, *Man's Search for Meaning*, Quotes of famous people, accessed June 9, 2021, https://quotepark.com/authors/viktor-e-frankl/quotes-about-freedom/.

is the catch: the end destination is unknown. "Just pack up and go to a land that I will show you." Which way was he expected to head out? How much provisioning did he require to take with him? How long was the journey? You see, sometimes we are required to step out in belief and go to the land that Yahweh will show us. It requires that we take the first step and be courageous in our actions. Only then are we able to please Elohim, for "without belief it is impossible to please Him" (Hebrews 11:6). Sometimes the road trip means getting into a car and heading out to an unknown destination for an unspecified time because only then will Elohim show us where we need to go and what we need to do.

> *I once heard this great testimony of a gentleman who was told by Elohim to go and take Bibles to a village in a very isolated part of the mountains in a distant country. The man did as he was commanded; he bought a vehicle in a neighboring country, bought Bibles, then put them in the car. This was a dangerous undertaking as the country he was travelling to was not friendly to Christians. Nevertheless, he did as he was told. When he got to the border post, he was asked what he was doing. He told the border guards that he was going to deliver books to this specific village, and even though the Bibles were clearly visible in the car, the border guards waved him through. As he continued on his journey, he had to travel through a mountain pass. The car broke down irreparably, and he was stranded on the mountainside. A few long hours passed, when a man from the village where he was going to approached him and asked him if he was the man who had the books for them. This is incredible, for the delivery man had not made any contact with the village at all; he just knew that he was required to deliver the Bibles. When the delivery man asked what books the villager was referring to, the*

> *villager replied that it was the books that explained about the man who died on the cross. Each of the villagers had had a dream that told them the books were coming. The end of the story is that the Bibles were delivered to the villagers.*

When called to set out on a journey, go. Be prepared to step out in belief. The One who sent you will send His Comforter, the Spirit of Elohim, to be your travel companion and guide. Sometimes going to the land that will be shown to you is not the only option … it is the best one.

Belief

What happens when something really bad happens to us? What do we do when something monumentally disastrous happens to us? How do we cope? What do we do? We need to *believe* in Elohim, not *for* anything but just *in* Him. When we believe, we "know that all matters work together for good to those who love Elohim, to those who are called according to his purpose" (Romans 8:28). We also believe the Word of Elohim when it says that we will never "be tried beyond what you are able, but with the trial shall also make the way of escape, enabling you to bear it" (1 Corinthians 10:13). See, when we believe, this is what we believe. We also believe that we can do all things through Messiah who strengthens us (see Philippians 4:13). This is what belief does: it allows us to believe in Him for our well-being instead of depending on ourselves and on others. If we believe in the Word of Elohim and live out that belief, then we will live the life of abundance that has been promised to us in the Word. That belief requires action because belief without works is dead. So, we are going to face trials of many kinds, and we "count it all joy" when we do because we know that our suffering will lead to perseverance and endurance, our perseverance to hope, and hope to character. (See James 1:2-4 and Romans 5:3-5.) "Count it all joy." This we can believe, for it is written so.

I want to share the following with you regarding the difference between faith and belief, according to definition. It is important to note that there is a big difference between the two, which gives it the power and the meaning.

- *Faith* is a complete trust or confidence in someone or something. This means that we can have faith in someone who has produced on their word or delivered on their promises, or, for example, have faith in equipment that we use for climbing or other potentially dangerous or even safe activities.

- *Belief* is an acceptance that a statement is true or that something exists. This means that we accept that it is the truth, even though we have not yet seen it. For example, we believe in the Spirit of Elohim and Yahweh and Yeshua Messiah. None of us have actually "seen" Them, but we have experienced the fullness of Their power in operation.

There is a big difference between faith and belief, yet we use these two words as if they were the same thing. Even by worldly standards, there is a difference between the two, and I want you to be very clear on what the world says and what the Word says. Yeshua Himself said the He is "the Way, and the *Truth*, and the Life" (John 14:6) ... we need to accept that what the Word says is the absolute truth, because it is.

Power of Words
I want to impress upon you here the power of words. It might sound like I am being a little nit-picky, but if you read the Word of Elohim, then you will understand that we need to be nit-picky in our use of them. The book of James is very explicit concerning the tongue. James 3:6 says, "And the tongue is a fire, the world of unrighteousness. Among our members the tongue is set, the one defiling the entire body, and setting on fire the wheel of life, and it is set on fire by GeHinnom [Hell]." This is quite profound as we can see that the tongue, which utters the words we speak, is quite a powerful tool. In the previous verse James says, "The tongue is a little member, yet boasts greatly. See how a little fire kindles a great forest!" The passage then goes on to say in verse 8 that "no man is able to tame the tongue. It is unruly, evil, filled with deadly poison."

The book of Proverbs is the best source of wisdom; it has much to say regarding the tongue and the words we speak. In chapter 18 it says that "death and life are in the power of the tongue, and those loving it eat its fruit" (verse 21). We should be very careful of what we say and of what words we use because with them come the power of death and life. If we face a situation with a choice of death and life, we should always choose life.

Count the Cost
We then need to count the cost of this trip. What will it cost us to go on this journey? There is always a cost. Sometimes it is a financial one and other times it is a non-material cost. Remember that in order to reach the goal of losing weight, we need to make some sacrifices. Too often we are not prepared to pay the cost of what we want to achieve. Consider the rich young ruler who came to Yeshua and asked Him what he needed to do in order to inherit everlasting life. Yeshua responded by telling him to sell all that he had, give it to the poor, and follow Him. The rich young man left grieved because he was unwilling to pay the price. (Read Matthew 19:16-22.) The cost of wholeness can be harsh and hard, but it is not impossible. It is written that "with men this is impossible, but with Elohim all is possible" (Matthew 19:26). That means everything! Nothing is excluded from this statement, but we have to believe. We need the belief of a mustard seed, and then we will be able to "say to the mountain, 'Move from here to there,' and it shall move. And no matter shall be impossible for you" (Matthew 17:20). The cost is possible because the price has already been paid—the price that you and I would never have been able to pay or will ever be able to repay even if we tried. We need to count the cost of living in belief; we have free rein to do what we want, but we will never be free from suffering the consequences of our choices and our actions. We can choose to believe or not to believe, but we will not escape the consequences. If we choose to believe, then we walk in the freedom and abundance of our choice. When we choose not to believe, then we will be slaves to bondage and suffer infirmities of every kind. We have the freedom of choice, but we are never free from their consequences.

> *"I have set before you life and death, the blessing and the curse. Therefore you shall choose life, so that you live, both you and your seed" (Deuteronomy 30:19).*

We should choose life so that we may live life and live it in abundance. Count the cost before undertaking the journey. If you choose not to go on the journey to become whole, then chances are that your desire for wholeness was not enough, and you will fail as a result.

Stop and Refuel

When undertaking this journey, you will need to stop and refuel, especially if the journey is long. We need to resupply so that we can continue on and reach our destination. Life is like this, too; we need to take time out to stop, reflect and replenish. We need to refuel for the rest of the journey so that we can continue and be successful in our lives. Even Yeshua took time to do this. He often went off on His own to replenish and refuel. It is written that "those who wait on יהוה renew their strength" (Isaiah 40:31), and this is what Yeshua did: He waited on Yahweh. We need to do the same. We need to wait on Him and be expectant of the promised outcome even though we have not yet seen it. Refuelling or recharging is an important part of this journey because it allows us to take stock of where we are, what we have done and how well we are doing. It allows us to take a breath and get ready for the next part of the journey. We need fuel to complete this journey.

Your desire to achieve must be coupled to joy.

Firstly, you need fuel to get you from one place to another; when your fuel runs out, you are unable to continue. Most worldly fuel sources have a relatively short life span, and once they are done, you need to find more fuel or more sources. Your desire to succeed is fueled by either love or hatred. You will either love what you are doing or hate it. It is written in Matthew 6:24 that "no one is able to serve two masters, for either he shall hate the one and love the other, or else he shall cleave to the one and despise the other." The verse ends with, "You are not able to serve Elohim and mammon [the devil]." Where does this fuel come from? It will come from one of two sources: from Elohim above or from the devil below. There is a choice to be made, and it does not happen automatically; the right choice has to be developed, nurtured and fed. Without fuel we are not going anywhere—or we will only go as far as the fuel we have. Your desire will drive you to achieve your goal, but desire is not enough. It has to be coupled to joy. "For the joy of יהוה is your strength" (Nehemiah 8:10).

> *Many years ago, I had the privilege of attending a Bible school, and I can clearly remember the one teaching that has stayed with me to this day: the teaching of joy. The instructor told us that in the last days, which are now, many will fall away from Elohim because they will have no joy. The joy, the fruit of the Spirit which is our strength, will fade, and we will give up. That teaching has been a pillar of my life for many years now.*

The second thing, which may not seem to be relevant here but needs mentioning, is that we need to learn to cook our own food. In other words, we need to be able to study the Word of Elohim and allow the Spirit of Elohim to teach us what we need to learn without relying on somebody else to do it for us. The Spirit of Elohim is our Teacher, our Guide and our Comforter (look up John 14:26 in different translations), and we need to allow Him to lead us in our lives. The refuelling process is clearly spelled out for us in Isaiah 40:31, which says that "those who wait on Yahweh renew their strength." We have to wait and spend time in His presence, be filled with His Spirit, so that we are refueled for the journey. Then we will run and not be weary and we will walk and not faint, as Isaiah 40:31 says.

Detours and Roadblocks

On this journey we will encounter some detours and roadblocks; not all of it is going to be smooth sailing. We will have to endure bad roads and sometimes seemingly endless traffic. This is part of the journey. At times we will want to abandon this journey because of the roadblocks. But we need to persevere on this trip, and occasionally we will need to stop and do running repairs. This is all part of the experience, and if you think it won't be like that, then you are deceiving yourself. Life is not perfect, and we cannot expect it to be so; we have to understand and be prepared for these needs. We have to know that there will be times when things are rough. However, we have been equipped to deal with these things. It is written that "His Mighty-like power [the Spirit of Elohim] has given to us all we need for life and reverence, through the knowledge of Him who called us to esteem and uprightness" (2 Peter 1:3).

You see, we need to have the knowledge of Him to live this life, and we are commanded to add to this knowledge things that are important to us according to Elohim. Having this knowledge means we can apply it in times of need.

> *For example, suppose you have a flat tire. When you know how to change the tire and have the right equipment to do so, then the task becomes easy. But when you do not have the knowledge or the tools to do the job, then you will battle and ultimately fail.*

We are commanded, in 2 Peter 1, to "add to your belief uprightness, to uprightness knowledge, to knowledge self-control, to self-control endurance, to endurance reverence, to reverence brotherly affection, and to brotherly affection love" (verses 5-7).

We have to do all of these things; they will not be done for us. We need to equip ourselves for this journey so that, according to the next verse, if these things "are in you and increase, they cause you to be neither inactive nor without fruit in the knowledge of our Master, Yeshua Messiah" (2 Peter 1:8). We will encounter detours and roadblocks and obstacles, and we need to be equipped to deal with them. According to the previous passage of scripture, Elohim has given us everything we need. Plus, when the Word says that we will never "be tried [tested] beyond what you are able, but with the trial shall also make the way of escape, enabling you to bear it" (1 Corinthians 10:13), then it is so! And if we "have strength to do all, through Messiah who empowers me" (Philippians 4:13), then it is so!

We are now ready for this journey and set out on our trip, but we soon encounter some problems on the road. Sometimes it is a minor setback and sometimes it is a major setback, but each setback or obstacle has been placed there so that we can *deal* with it. Occasionally these obstacles come at just the wrong time, when we are being overwhelmed by everything all at once. Most of the time an obstacle appears because we failed to deal with it the first time it happened and we put it off for another day. You know, it's the "I don't have time for it right now" scenario. Well, there is no other good time like the present to deal with it. When things go wrong—and they will—we are to tend to the problem right there and then, so that we can deal with the issue and get it out of the way quickly. We often procrastinate in our efforts because we lack the zeal and the desire to deal with the problem; we would rather cover it up and hope that it disappears on its own. This will not happen to most of the problems we face, as then they will be allowed to fester, spoil and become rotten and will affect our health in every way.

Much the same way, when a little bit of damage happens to a healthy apple, if that spot is not cut out, it will soon grow and destroy the whole apple. But if the rotten piece is cut out, then we can still enjoy the fruit.

Two things are at play here. One is knowing that there is a problem and what the problem is, and the second is having the tools and the knowledge to fix said problem.

For example, that flat tire on the vehicle is quite simple to identify because we can see the damage and feel the result of the flat while driving. If we have a spare and the necessary tools to replace the tire, then it is an easy fix. I have seen many a driver with a flat tire stranded on the side of the road with all the tools available to fix it, but with no practical application skills to get the job done. There are also those who have no idea of what the problem is, let alone an idea of how to fix it, who have to call for roadside assistance. While calling for roadside assistance is not a big deal, there are things in life we should learn to do on our own. We should learn to "cook our own food," as I said before. However, sometimes the problem is mechanical or electrical and there is no way for us to fix it. We will have to call roadside assistance, and then this is the best option to take.

Think of life as this road trip. Sometimes when we have a "flat tire" along the way, we want to get angry or annoyed and call for roadside assistance even though we should be able to fix the problem on our own. Sometimes the problem is bigger than we can deal with, so we need some assistance, which is the Spirit of Elohim and the manual we use with all the knowledge of how to deal with things, called the Word of Elohim. Sometimes we need some specific matter dealt with, and then we need the "mechanic," the Spirit of Elohim, in order for us to be repaired. A lot of time these breakdowns occur at moments when we need them the least and in places where other help is not readily available—like being stranded in the middle of a long stretch of desert road with no cell phone coverage and very little traffic coming through.

Wilderness
Sometimes we are purposely led into the wilderness by Elohim so that we can learn and grow and become prepared for the next phase of our journey. If Yeshua was led "into the wilderness" by the Spirit "to be tried [tempted] by the devil" (Matthew 4:1), you can count on it that you and I will have the same experience. You should ask yourself, why did this happen? Why would Yeshua be tempted by the devil? I believe it was to prove to us, and to His Father, that the power of the Spirit was all we needed to defeat the devil. Also in Matthew 3:13-17, just prior to Him going into the wilderness, Yeshua was baptized (immersed) in water and the Spirit of Elohim descended down from heaven like a dove and came upon Him. What is awesome about it is that Yahweh publicly recognizes His Son by saying, "This is My Son, the Beloved, in whom I delight" (verse 17). So Yeshua, full of the Spirit of Elohim, is led into the wilderness to be tempted by the devil. Yeshua, who had the power of the Spirit of Elohim in Him, is sent on this journey into the wilderness.

EMOTIONAL WHOLENESS

This is not a luxury cruise here. It is not on the road well-travelled; it is harsh territory filled with obstacles and danger. But, Yeshua is on it, armed and equipped and ready for the journey. His fuel was the Spirit of Elohim, which had given Him everything He needed for life and for reverence. Yeshua had everything He needed for this journey, and He applied this knowledge when it was needed. When He was tempted by the devil, Yeshua did not try and have discourse with him. He did not try and explain some things to the devil; He did not try and convince the devil; instead, He spoke the truth to the devil. Yeshua told the devil what the Word of Elohim said. Yeshua took the tool, the Word of Elohim, and wielded it with knowledge and authority, like it should be, so that He could stand firm in the truth and power of it.

You and I should do the same. We, too, will be led into the wilderness from time to time to build our faith. We will suffer in the wilderness in order to persevere and to develop character so that we can have hope. I believe that 1 Thessalonians 1:3 sums this up very well:

> *"Remembering without ceasing your work of the belief, and the labour of love, and the endurance of the expectation in our Master יהושע Messiah in the presence of our Elohim and Father."*

The New International Version states 1 Thessalonians 1:3 this way:

> *"We remember before our God and Father your work produced by faith, your labor prompted by love, and your endurance inspired by hope in our Lord Jesus Christ."*

See clearly what it says: we remember, without stopping, our work, produced by our belief; our work, or labor, driven no less than by love; and the endurance of our belief in Yeshua Messiah—in Him, not *for* anything, but just *in* Him. Everything we do—our labor—driven by love, with the endurance of our belief in Yeshua in the presence of Elohim our Father, is our goal. It is what will drive us on this journey to wholeness without giving up.

From Brokenness to Wholeness

I am reminded of a man whose wife was sick with a certain illness. He himself was a pastor and had prayed for his wife on many occasions, but she had not recovered. He had prayed for other people with the same illness, and they had been healed by Elohim. This was frustrating and annoying to him, and he fought with Elohim about this matter, to no avail. Many years passed, and on a certain day the pastor decided to quit the ministry and go on retirement. Elohim told him to enjoy the last few hours of his life with his wife because he was not going to last long after retirement. This struck a very deep chord with the pastor, whose prayer was that he would fear Elohim because the fear of Elohim is the beginning of all wisdom (see Proverbs 9:10)—and these words from Elohim had caused him great fear. This pastor had persevered for many years with this prayer, and he decided there and then that it was not a good idea to retire. His prayer was answered right there, and the fear of Elohim struck him where it mattered most. Long story short, he repented of his anger and frustration toward Elohim, and the day after this encounter his wife was prayed for by another pastor at the same event, and this time his wife was healed. But it took many years and lots of prayer and supplication and petition for this healing to happen. This pastor had said that the work had to be done in him first before Elohim could do the work in her.

I tell this story so that we can understand and put into context the power of the Word of Elohim. This pastor had suffered through the illness of his wife, not physically as much as mentally and spiritually, because he loved his wife and hated to see her suffer. His love for his wife drove him to persevere for her health. Elohim developed the pastor's character through this ordeal; when he got to the point of breaking, it was time to execute the miracle. Too often we want instant gratification and become despondent when things don't go our way. But this pastor, at the brink of resignation, gets his prayer answered—and the fear of Elohim overtook him to the point that he decided to continue serving Elohim. His belief in Elohim was restored and his desire to serve Elohim was invigorated, so much so that Elohim healed his wife. It was not about the healing; it was about the love for Elohim and the belief in Him alone. Love drove this pastor to the point of desperation, and it is often at this point that Elohim is able to step in and do the things that we have been trying to do for years.

Team

The next aspect of the journey is who is going with you. Who goes with you is important because this journey should not be done alone. Yeshua, who was the Son of Yahweh, when He was on earth, did not go on this journey alone. He gathered together a group of men known as the twelve disciples, who traveled with Yeshua wherever He went. At no time did Yeshua decide that it was best to go it alone. He always had someone with Him, and furthermore, from the twelve He had three who were the closest to Him, and even then there was one with whom He had a special relationship: John. Even Yeshua knew the value of having people on this trip with Him; He knew that He needed their assistance to get things done. We have been conditioned by the world to be strong, independent people, to do things on our own and not rely on others for help because they will always disappoint or let us down. However, we should be strong, *interdependent* people. Let us no longer be conformed to the patterns of this world but be transformed by the renewing of our minds (see Romans 12:2). When we have the right team assembled, then we are able to do the things we ought to and be successful in life. Just as the disciples were a team for the Messiah that got things done together, so we also should have a team of people who can help us on this road trip. We often want to go it alone, but there is a huge danger in that, for when we are isolated and get into trouble, we are unable to stand against the onslaught. The Spirit of Elohim has been given to us so that we will never be alone and never be lonely and always have some direction in which to travel.

Accountability

Another great reason to have good travel companions is that there is safety in numbers; there is an accountability in a group that does not exist in a single person.

Think of nature and you will see that most animals congregate in herds because it provides them with safety. The predators try and isolate a member of a herd into a single unit so that it is easier to drag it down and kill it. When we are isolated, we are easy targets, vulnerable and open to attack. The predator will always try to get us on our own, then show us our weaknesses and make us feel ashamed of ourselves, to the point where we don't share things with anyone. By doing that, he, the devil, is able to separate us and so steal, slaughter and destroy (see John 10:10).

> *I know of a group of leaders at a big church who were all suffering from addiction to pornography and had formed this group to help and support each other. Each time one of the members watched some pornography, he would text the group a single word. The other members of the group would then intercede on behalf of the confessing member or phone with words of encouragement as they were led of the Spirit. This happened on a regular basis in the beginning, but as the power of the Spirit took over and the victories in these people's lives was realized, the need for constant texting subsided, to be replaced by victory.*

This is the power of good, accountable people on your road trip. Now, the Word does say to "confess your trespasses to one another, and pray for one another, so that you are healed" (James 5:16). There is power in obedience to the Word of Elohim and in the practical application of this truth. Accountability is not a big stick to be used to beat others who are struggling with some affliction; rather, it is a gentle rod of correction that is used to guide and bring a person back into right standing with Elohim. The devil will bring shame and guilt upon us to keep us isolated so that we do not see the light of the gospel. When there is guilt and shame, believe that it is the work of the devil; Yahweh, the mighty Elohim, will never, ever let you feel guilt and shame.

> *This was one of the things that kept me back when I first was born again. I had had a terrible private life and had made many, many mistakes. The guilt and shame that I experienced stopped me from enjoying the fullness of life that was given to me. I constantly was beating myself up because of the lie that I was never going to be good enough because of my past. I had to believe the truth—that I had been redeemed, which means I had been bought back and relieved of all debt, that I had been "re-bought." Fortunately, I had a good friend and mentor who was able to gently guide me to this truth, and I experienced a great freedom in this area of my life.*

Now, this sounds simple, but it is only when you understand and believe you have been redeemed that you will be truly set free from the captivity in your mind. It makes no sense to us that we do not have to repay this debt—which we never could anyway because the price is so far above what we are able to pay—because we are so indoctrinated by this world that we have to pay for what we have received. It is difficult for us to freely receive because we think we are not worthy of receiving or of being redeemed. This is a lie from the pit of hell, and if we fail to believe this very thing, then nothing else will matter.

Guilt and shame are from the devil, while conviction of sin is from Elohim.

Guilt is from the devil; conviction is from Elohim.

There are times when going on your own is required, but you will know when because the Spirit of Elohim will tell you. John the Baptist spent fourteen years in the wilderness being prepared; Yeshua spent forty days and nights in the wilderness on His own. There will be times when you, too, will be on your own, but never alone, and you will never be lonely if you have the right direction to travel toward. Remember that loneliness is not the absence of affection, but the absence of direction.

Failure
Sometimes we will fail at achieving the end result, of reaching the destination that we set out for. Is it because we are useless and cannot succeed? Or is it because we were never destined to go there in the first place? Sometimes it is because we were never destined to be there in the first place. We go on our own paths without a plan and hope to receive the blessings of our own choices, but that will never happen because we are not in the desire of Elohim. We cannot expect to be blessed when we are disobedient, much in the same way that we never reward our children when they are disobedient towards us.

Failure also can be the result of poor choices we make while expecting a great result. Some silly examples are to want to score well on a test but decide to go out all night with friends instead of studying or to want to win an upcoming race but decide to eat unhealthy foods and drink too much beforehand. These choices definitely lead to failure, so we cannot be surprised or disappointed when failure happens as a result. What about life choices we make that lead to bad endings—are we failures, or have we just failed? Think about this for a moment. Are we failures, or have we just failed, meaning are we, as people, failures? Are we just a waste of human life? Has Elohim wasted His time creating us? Or have we just failed because we were ill-equipped for the task or had a lack of knowledge in the field we were trying to succeed in?

We are not failures; we have been created by Elohim to be "perfect and straight" (Job 1:1) and "before Him, in love" (Ephesians 1:4). How does that equate to failure? We have been blinded by the devil to believe that we are failures and that we will never be good enough to achieve anything. Now, while this may be so in and of ourselves, it is absolutely contrary to the Word of Elohim. It is written:

> ***"For you were bought with a price, therefore esteem Elohim in your body and in your spirit, which are of Elohim" (1 Corinthians 6:20).***

We are no longer slaves but sons (children) of Elohim (see Galatians 4:7), and I am sure that if we are sons of Elohim, then surely we are not failures. The devil will tell us time and time again that we are failures, and while it seems like the truth, it is the furthest thing from it. We must choose as to who we are going to believe: Elohim or the devil. We cannot serve two masters because we will love the one and hate the other or be devoted to one and despise the other (see Matthew 6:24). We have to make life choices. When we make death choices, we will surely fail.

We also can fail because we do not pay the price for achieving the goal. We want things to happen for the good, but we are not willing to put in the hard work to achieve the goal. Again, the simple example is somebody who desperately needs to lose weight but is unwilling to give up the bad eating habits and laziness to go to the gym and exercise or to eat properly.

When we don't pay the price, we will never achieve the goals we set for ourselves. Often the desire to succeed is overridden by our desire to be lazy or complacent. We lack the desire to be healthy or to be whole and instead bask in our laziness, complacency or apathy—only to complain when things do not work out in our lives. Failure is an option when we do not want to pay the price for making good choices. Things don't just happen on their own; they are caused.

We become fat and lazy because we eat unhealthily and don't exercise. We become emotionally damaged because we don't spend time in becoming whole, and yes, we need to spend time doing so.

Wholeness is a result of dedication and devotion to the Word of Elohim and to a relationship with Him. Wholeness is the end result of a process, not a quick fix or get-well-now scheme. We fail because we are not willing to pay the price. The rich young ruler in Mark 10 left Yeshua after being told the cost of entering into the kingdom of heaven. He was unwilling to pay the price, so he failed. You and I are in the same boat. We need to pay the price for success, but if we are unwilling to do so, we will fail. Wholeness comes with a price.

There is a big difference between failing and being a failure. We are not destined to be failures, but we do fail. It reminds me of a song in which the singer says, "People say I'm strange, does it make me a stranger."[2] So if I fail, does that make me a failure? No, it does not.

> *Take this example. If I decided to start a business in automotive engineering and poured thousands upon thousands of dollars into the business and thousands of man hours in getting it set up, I would fail miserably. Is it because I am a failure? No, it is because I am not an automotive engineer and have no business background. I therefore set myself up for failure. I would have nobody else to blame except myself because I had made really poor choices in starting this business. If, on the other hand, I did the same thing but had an experienced business partner and an experienced automotive engineer, then I would have more chance of success because I had made better choices.*

We cannot blame anyone but ourselves for our failures. The world is not against us, as some would believe; we just make bad choices that result in failure. So it is with us in life. We fail at things because we make poor life choices that result in death rather than life, and we try and do things that we should not do or are not trained and equipped to do.

---

2 Toby McKeehan and Mark Heimermann, "Jesus Freak," song, 1995, dc Talk album "Jesus Freak."

Chapter Five
The Helper

The Role of the Set-Apart (Holy) Spirit
We need to believe that when the Set-Apart Spirit reveals things to us, we need to do something about them. We need to recognize and understand His authority in these things and allow Him to have His way in our lives. There are a few vital roles of the Set-Apart Spirit that we need to know and understand so that we have the knowledge and authority in our lives to use for the kingdom of Elohim. Read John 14 and 16, Romans 8 and 15, 1 Corinthians 12, and Ephesians 1 and you will find:

1. He is a helper and a reminder because He has been sent to teach us all things and to bring to remembrance all the things that we have been taught.
2. He convicts us of sin and righteousness and judgment.
3. He dwells in us and empowers us every day.
4. He is the source of revelation, wisdom and power. He is the very same power that raised Yeshua from the dead, and we would do well to believe this.
5. He guides us into all truth.

6. He gives us spiritual gifts to use.
7. He is a seal for the believers … not the unbelievers.
8. He is a helper in the time of weakness.
9. He renews us and gives us eternal life.
10. He sanctifies us. In other words, He sets us apart from others and declares us holy.

We can see that He, the Set-Apart Spirit of Elohim, has a wide number of tasks to fulfill in our lives, if we let Him. When we are filled with the Set-Apart Spirit, He is able to do the things that He has been tasked to do. When we ask Him to show us areas of our lives that need attention, He will do so. He will lead us into all truth; He will help us in our weakness; and He will empower us with the same power that raised Yeshua from the dead, so that we can accomplish what we need to accomplish. I cannot stress this enough. We need to believe, and we need to act on what we believe, for without that belief it is impossible to please Elohim (see Hebrews 11:6).

> *"For Elohim so loved the world that He gave His only brought-forth Son, so that everyone who believes in Him should not perish but possess everlasting life" (John 3:16).*

The Fruit of the Spirit

> *"But the fruit of the Spirit is love, joy, peace, patience, kindness, goodness, trustworthiness, gentleness, self-control. Against such there is no Torah" (Galatians 5:22-23).*

The Word of Elohim has much to say about seed. Thus it is important that we understand the process of how seeds grow. Then we can know, have knowledge of, its operation in our lives.

Luke 8 records a parable in which Yeshua tells the large crowd about the sower who "went out to sow his seed. And as he sowed, some indeed fell by the wayside. And it was trodden down, and the birds of the heaven devoured it. And other fell on rock, and when it grew up, it withered because it had no moisture. And other fell among thorns, and the thorns grew up with it and choked it. And other fell on the good soil, and grew up, and yielded a crop a hundredfold" (Luke 8:5-8). The disciples of Yeshua asked Him what He meant by this parable. Yeshua explained the parable in this way:

> *"The seed is the word of Elohim. And those by the wayside are the ones who hear, then the devil comes and takes away the word from their hearts, lest having believed, they should be saved. And those on the rock are those who, when they hear, receive the word with joy. And these have no root, who believe for a while and in time of trial fall away. And that which fell among thorns are those who, when they have heard, go out and are choked with worries, and riches, and pleasures of life, and bring no fruit to perfection. And that on the good soil are those who, having heard the word with a noble and good heart, retain it, and bear fruit with endurance" (Luke 8:11-15).*

This is a very powerful parable as it illustrates what we are to do with the seed that has been planted in us. In order for there to be fruit, there has to be a seed, and this seed has to be planted in us so that it can grow. But, as we see in the parable, there are conditions that need to be met in order for the seed to grow into a good crop. When a farmer goes to sow seed, he does not simply go to a field and spread seed around it, hoping that it will be successful. No, first he prepares the soil, getting it ready for the seed.

This is what happens in our lives. The gardener, Yahweh, sends His Spirit to prepare our soil, our hearts, to receive the seed, and then the seed is planted in us. The first seed is the seed that allows us to see that He, Yahweh, so loved the world that He sent His only Son so that whoever believes in Him will not perish but have everlasting life (see John 3:16). Without this seed, we will never see Yeshua as the truth and the way and the life (see John 14:6); we will forever be in darkness and have no hope. Once this seed is planted, then the soil in our hearts determines the outcome of the plant. If we are on the wayside, then the devil will come and take the seed away from our hearts so that we don't believe and won't be saved. If our hearts are stone, then the seed will take root but will wither and die because there is no moisture. There is nothing that feeds us and nurtures us, so we wither and die. If we are those whose seed has fallen between the thorns, then the seed will grow but will be choked out by worries and riches and pleasures of life and bring no fruit to perfection. Our lives are like this. When the seed of the Spirit is planted in our lives, we are the ones who decide what to do with the seed. If our hearts are by the wayside, then the seed will be eaten by the evil one and will never come to fruition.

The outcome of the seed is our decision.

We get to decide the outcome of this planting. The seed is planted because this is Elohim's desire for us. We make the decisions that determine the outcome of the seed. When we decide to believe that Yahweh sent His Son for us and confess it with our mouths, then the heart of stone we have is made new and is changed. It is written in Ezekiel that He will give us "one heart, and put a new spirit within you"; He will take our heart of stone out of our flesh and give us a new heart of flesh (11:19). Then He will put His Spirit in us, and He shall cause us to "walk in My laws, and guard My right-rulings, and shall do them" (Ezekiel 11:20). We need to have a new heart in order to receive the Spirit of Elohim; otherwise, we will be like the seed that is sown between the weeds or on the rocks.

When we try and live two lives—one for Elohim and one in the world—the weeds will choke the life and we will be choked out. Think of the weeds in a garden: when they are not removed, they overrun the good grass and plants and destroy the garden. The same is true for us. We think that we can handle both sides of the fence when it is impossible to do so. We cannot serve two masters;

we will either love the one and hate the other or we will serve the one and despise the other, as Matthew 6:24 says. Or, in another part of scripture, we cannot make a fire in our bosom (lap) and not expect our clothes to get burnt (see Proverbs 6:27). And, there is no fellowship between light and darkness (see 2 Corinthians 6:14). So it is with the seed of Elohim. We either tend to the garden and remove the weeds or the weeds will overtake us and destroy us. Pause here for a moment again to hear what is written: the seed that is among thorns are those who "go out and are choked with worries, and riches, and pleasures of life, and bring no fruit to perfection" (Luke 8:14). Is it any wonder that we are commanded to not be anxious over anything? If we are disobedient to this command, then we will be choked out. It is as simple as that. So, the seed that is sown is our responsibility. We are to tend it, nurture it and make sure that it produces a great crop in season. We are to have good and noble hearts and retain the Word of Elohim so that we can bring the fruit to perfection.

All of the fruits of the Spirit are planted in us as seeds, and we are responsible for the nurturing and tending of these seeds. We are commanded clearly how to do this: we are to remain in the vine, with Elohim as the master gardener and we as the branches.

If we stay in the vine, then we will be tended to and pruned and nurtured so that we can bear good fruit in season. But if we fail to remain, then we are cut off and left to dry, to be thrown into the fire to be burnt (see John 15:6).

We seem to think that we have no responsibility in this matter, but this is false and is a complete lie. It is written:

> *"Blessed is the man who shall not walk in the counsel of the wrong, and shall not stand in the path of sinners. And shall not sit in the seat of scoffers, but his delight is in the Torah [law] of יהוה, and he meditates in His Torah day and night. For he shall be as a tree planted by the rivers of water, that yields its fruit in its season, and whose leaf does not wither, and whatever he does prospers" (Psalm 1:1-3).*

Yeshua said:

> *"If anyone thirsts, let him come to Me, and let him who believes in Me drink. As the Scripture said, out of His innermost shall flow rivers of living water"* (John 7:37-38).

Now that we have had a look at the role of the Set-Apart Spirit, we need to see what the evidence of Him is. Simply put, we cannot be filled with the Spirit of Elohim and not bear any fruit or not have any evidence of Him in our lives. A fruit tree that has been planted, it must be nurtured and tended to, pruned and cared for, in order for it to bear any fruit in season. It is the same with the Spirit of Elohim in us. We must take great care of the seed planted in us and tend to it so that we may bear the fruit thereof; it will not happen on its own accord. We are responsible for this process. Having said that, let us have a look at what the fruit of the Spirit of Elohim is.

> *"But the fruit of the Spirit is love, joy, peace, patience, kindness, goodness, trustworthiness, gentleness, self-control"* (Galatians 5:22-23).

Love
We have already spoken at length about the power and importance of love and what it did and is meant to do for us. Love is the very foundation of Yahweh and the very foundation for this book. Without it, we are doomed to fail.

Joy
Joy is not an emotion; it cannot be fabricated or faked and is not dependant on our circumstances in life. We can be in the worst place in our lives but still have joy if we know clearly in which direction we are headed. This is in stark contrast to happiness, which is a result of emotions. Joy is from the Spirit of Elohim, given to us so that we can have the strength to persevere and push through.

Peace
This is the peace that "surpasses all human understanding" (Philippians 4:7) and is in direct opposition to anxiety and "dis-ease." When we are full of the Spirit of Elohim, we will have this peace that goes beyond any level of our comprehension.

Patience
A famous evangelist gave a description of patience, saying that patience is not the ability to wait, since we all have to wait; rather, it is the attitude we display while waiting.[1] While we are on this journey, we need to have the right attitude as we wait on Elohim for our healing.

Kindness
This a fruit that we sadly lack in the world today. We are so desperate at times to look after ourselves that we fail to look out for others needier than us. Kindness can be described as the attitude we have that delights in contributing to the well-being of others. It is impossible to consider others when we lack this vital fruit.

Goodness
Goodness in man is not a mere passive quality; rather, it is the deliberate preference of right to wrong, the firm and persistent resistance against all moral evil, and the choosing and following of all spiritual and moral excellence. We can never be perfect, but we can strive to be excellent.

Trustworthiness
Trustworthiness means that we are able to be trusted, that people have a confidence in us based on our deeds and word. It means that our yes is yes and our no is no and that we are the same every day in our deeds and word. This does not mean that we won't have off days, but it does mean that we will be consistent in our actions.

---

[1] Joyce Meyer, *Battlefield of the Mind* (New York: Warner Books, 1995).

Gentleness

This fruit means that we have a softness of manners, a mildness of temper and a kind character. The way we deal with things is a reflection of this gentleness, which is often lacking when we are hurt and broken.

Self-control

Self-control is self-explanatory; it means we have control over ourselves in what we think, say and do. The basis of this word means mastery of self, and the Spirit of Elohim gives us this ability. We need to exercise it daily and become masters of ourselves in the process.

As you can see, the fruit of the Spirit of Elohim is extremely vital in our day-to-day journey, and without it, we are left powerless and useless to do anything. We have been given the opportunity to have the fruit of the Spirit, but we have to nurture these fruits and grow and develop them continuously. It is clearly stated in the Word that there is no law against these, meaning that when we have these fruits in abundance, we have no need for law (see Galatians 5:23). The more of the fruit of the Spirit we have, the less of our own mortal self will be in evidence. This passage concludes by saying that "if we live in the Spirit, let us also walk in the Spirit" (Galatians 5:25). This fruit will be needed in the journey from brokenness to wholeness if we are to have any chance of success.

Chapter Six
The Purpose of Revelation

Reveal

"... for flesh and blood has not revealed this to you, but My Father in the heavens" (Matthew 16:17).

Donald Rumsfeld coined the simple proverb that says we don't know what we don't know,[1] and this is a fact. We don't know what we don't know, and we often don't care to know for a number of reasons. We go through life wondering and wandering aimlessly because it suits us best. We use excuses to justify our unwillingness to deal with the obstacles. Please note that these obstacles are not just feelings and emotions, but powerful tools used by the devil to inflict pain and suffering and death in our lives. They are not harmless; they are very destructive.

In this chapter we are going to look at the first step in the process of achieving wholeness, and that is revelation. In order to fix something, we need to know it is broken. We need to know something needs fixing before we can even begin to move forward. Most people

---

[1] Donald Rumsfeld, *Known and Unknown* (New York: Sentinel, 2011).

will never have a revelation because a revelation is not desired. Most are not willing to ask the questions that need to be asked. We need to be bold and courageous in our approach as we move forward; we need to expect a great revelation in our lives so that we can be made whole. This is the vision of this book, that we "be perfect and complete, lacking in naught" (James 1:4).

There are a number of obstacles and reasons why we fail to have a revelation of what is wrong with our lives or what needs fixing. Mostly this lack of revelation is driven by fear, a fear of failure, and this fear is because we lack the love of Elohim. The Word clearly states that perfect love drives out all fear (see 1 John 4:18), so we fail because we don't have love. Other factors hinder us as well in this process, and we will deal with them later, but in order for revelation to work, we must have no fear and desire to be whole. We need to overcome these factors. We can do so only if we are prepared and well-equipped for the journey. Thankfully, the Spirit of Elohim has given us everything we need for life (see 2 Peter 1:3), and if we do as He says, then we will be victorious.

> *Back in early 2000, when I was in Canada, my life had been restored from being a hot mess and I had begun to heal from broken relationships with women. I remember asking Elohim one question that would radically change my life. The question was, why was my relationship with my mother so bad? Through the Spirit of Elohim, it was revealed to me that when I was eight years old and my parents separated, we children went to live with my mom, which I did not want to do. As a result, I started resenting my mom, and this resentment eventually turned to hatred and so much unforgiveness. It was because of my difficult relationship with my mother that my relationships with other women had been disastrous. Long story short, I asked God to forgive me of my unforgiveness, and when I returned to South Africa, I went to visit my mom and asked her to forgive me as well.*

The Purpose of Revelation

The release was overwhelming, and the relationship I have enjoyed with her over the past twenty years has been such a blessing. Best of all, when I tell this story to people battling with unforgiveness, I am always pleased to tell them how much my mother has changed as a result of the encounter: zero. My mother has not changed. I changed.

This story serves to highlight the power of revelation. When we ask Elohim for revelation, He will reveal to us what needs to be done. There is much need for revelation among believers today, but very little desire to have it, for reasons to be discussed shortly. However, in order for revelation to happen, several obstacles have to be overcome first before it can be fully appreciated and used. The "reveal" is just one small component of the puzzle that is essential to restoration and healing. Simply knowing, though, is not enough. The world will tell you that knowledge is power, but I strongly disagree. If knowledge was power, then we would not do half the stupid stuff that we do. Application of knowledge is where the real power lies.

Application of knowledge is the real power.

For example, suppose you are overweight. You can start reading all the material you like about eating healthy and exercising, and it will do nothing for you. Once you start *acting* on the knowledge is when the real change starts. So why do people not act on knowledge? What is the hindrance to their healing or their transformation?

Before any healing can take place, there needs to be a revelation of what is wrong. When we are unaware of what is wrong, when we don't know what we don't know, we will never change the way we think and the way we do. Also, we need to identify obstacles that might get in the way of our healing and then identify ways of dealing with those obstacles so that healing can take place in our lives.

Anger

Anger is defined as "a strong feeling of annoyance, displeasure or hostility."[2] Now, anger itself is not wrong; the fact that we don't deal with our anger is the problem. The Word of Elohim clearly states, "'Be wroth [angry], but do not sin.' Do not let the sun go down on your rage" (Ephesians 4:26). In other words, we are allowed to be angry, but we are not to sin when we are angry. Why, then, is anger an issue that needs to be dealt with? The reason is we allow anger to take hold in our hearts, which turns to resentment, which then turns to bitterness and hatred. This is the problem. We are taught in the Word of Elohim that when we have an issue with someone, we need to go and make it right with that person (see Matthew 18:15), and when we know that someone has an issue with us but is not coming to us to deal with it, then we need to go to that person and sort it out (see Matthew 5:23-24). So, anger in and of itself is not the problem; it is the unresolved anger that poses the big threat. Anger that is not dealt with eventually turns to bitterness and resentment and depression. I once read a piece—I don't remember exactly where—describing depression as frozen anger, which made sense because a lot of depression is caused by an event that harmed us and left us battered, bruised and hurting. We become angry to the point of depression because we feel hopeless and helpless.

Anxiety

Anxiety is defined as "a feeling of worry, nervousness or unease, typically about an imminent event or something with an uncertain outcome."[3] When we have done wrong and are covering it up, we become anxious about the possible outcome. We start worrying about the possible repercussions of and possible punishments for our actions. We become uneasy about ourselves and lose the peace that we are supposed to enjoy. Anxiety robs us of the quality of our lives that we should enjoy and instead gives us a whole host of other things that we were never designed to deal or cope with. We can develop a host of disorders, ranging from PTSD to depression to phobias, and none

---

2 Microsoft Bing, s.v. "anger," accessed June 10, 2021, https://www.bing.com/.
3 Microsoft Bing, s.v. "anxiety," accessed June 10, 2021, https://www.bing.com/.

of these are gifts or mechanisms designed to make us operate better and feel good about ourselves. Anxiety can lead to depression and depression to death. This is clearly the aim of the wicked one, except that he, the devil, gets us to do his dirty work for him. The Word of Elohim has clear warnings about anxiety and how to deal with it, and we should be obedient to the Word regarding it.

Denial

We like to deny the existence of any problems, saying that we are "great" and in "good shape" but denying that we need help. It makes us look weak if we acknowledge any problems, especially if we are in positions of authority where we have to be the best or on top of things.

> *Take, for example, a pastor heading up a church who battles with alcoholism. It would be seen as a weakness if he were to acknowledge that the problem exists and would put him in a bad light, so the denial sets in, fueled by the lie from the father of all lies. And so the pastor believes it and lives it.*

Denial is a dangerous thing and should be treated with the seriousness it deserves. There is no room for denial in our quest for wholeness. The consequences of being in denial are quite far-reaching, as it enables us to continue doing the wrong things or to remain engaged in harmful behaviors until it is too late. All too often we don't realize it until very late. "For all have sinned and fall short of the esteem of Elohim" (Romans 3:23). We need to stop denying and start acknowledging—that the Word of Elohim is the ultimate truth, the ultimate authority, and nothing else matters.

Fear

Synonyms of fear are "dread, fright, alarm, panic, terror, trepidation" and "mean, painful agitation in the presence or anticipation of danger."[4] "Fear" is the most general term and implies anxiety and

---

4 *Merriam-Webster's Collegiate Dictionary*, 11th ed., s.v. "fear."

usually loss of courage. We are more often than not driven or motivated by fear, and the biggest fear is the fear of failure—failure to meet the high standards expected of us by others, failure to meet the high standards set by ourselves, failure to achieve goals we have set, and so on. The list can be quite long and exhaustive, but suffice it to say that we are driven by fear and this fear leads to anxiety and, in the end, a loss of courage. When we get to this point in life, we are losing. At that point, life has lost its luster, and we no longer have a need to carry on or exist, which can lead to death. Fear will kill you more than death itself. But we were not given "a spirit of cowardice, but of power and of love and of self-control" (2 Timothy 1:7).

Guilt

Guilt is defined as a feeling of worry or unhappiness because you have done something wrong.[5] When we feel guilty, we start to worry about being caught, not necessarily about having done something wrong. We become unhappy because we have failed ourselves, our loved ones and others who regard us in high esteem. We cover up these feelings and pretend that everything is going well while struggling with the inner turmoil. We start believing the lie that we are no good, that we are not worthy, and that we do not deserve better in life because of what we have done. These feelings create within us a very strong feeling of unhappiness. Notice I say *feeling* again, not actual unworthiness but just the feeling … again. As with shame, guilt will destroy us to the point of death. Guilt and shame are from the devil. God does not make us feel guilty; He convicts us through the Spirit of Elohim, who leads us into all truth. Get rid of the guilt, declare it as a lie from the pit of hell, and repent from it. Ask and allow the Spirit of Elohim to lead you into the truth and show you what is the cause of your guilt.

Lack of Desire

When we have no desire to change, no desire to face our problems, or no desire to deal with whatever ails us, then we are not able to

---

5 Microsoft Bing, s.v. "guilt," accessed June 10, 2021, https://www.bing.com/.

persevere and push through the pain to reach the wholeness we were destined to have. The power of desire should never be underestimated in the pursuit of revelation. We fail to ask for revelation because we have no true desire to be healed.

Lack of Motivation

Motivation is defined as "the reason or reasons one has for acting or behaving in a particular way,"[6] so a lack of motivation then is the absence of a reason or reasons to behave in a certain way. What motivates us, and why are we motivated to do something? When there is a revelation about something, we are either motivated to do something or motivated not to. This motivation depends on whether something is done in love or in fear. When fear is our driver, our motivation quickly fades, and we lose the desire to press on and complete the goal or the task. When we are motivated by love, we endure to the end and accomplish the task at hand because our motivation is sound and secure. So, the Word of Elohim clearly tells us that we have not been given a "spirit of bondage again to fear" (Romans 8:15), but because we have fallen away from this truth and believe the world, we end up in fear. Motivation has to be driven by love in order to be pure and steadfast, to propel one to finish the course and reach the goal that has been set. If our motivation is driven by fear, we will fail miserably, and the consequence is death, on every level.

Lack of Self-Esteem

One of the biggest obstacles is a lack of self-esteem. The esteem we once had as little children might have been destroyed by loved ones or strangers who said or did things to us while we were growing up, to the point where we allowed any little bit of esteem we had to be totally demolished. I am saying *we* because we have control of our own emotions, we have control over our own esteem, based on our beliefs. Our lack of esteem has kept us from moving forward on many occasions because we believed that we were not good enough or worthy enough in ourselves. This obstacle, our lack of self-esteem, is

---

[6] Microsoft Bing, s.v. "motivation," accessed June 10, 2021, https://www.bing.com/.

often used by the devil against us. We are vulnerable because we have not yet begun to understand the value we have in Yahweh, our Elohim. When our esteem is based on our thoughts of ourselves or the thoughts of others about us, then we will surely fail. But when our esteem is based on the esteem of Yahweh of us, then we will not fail. We need a healthy self-esteem if we are to move forward from brokenness to a wholeness based on the Word of Elohim and not on man.

Pain

We are creatures of comfort by nature and very few of us actually enjoy pain in any form. We want to be healed of all the infirmities that we have, but we are not willing to deal with the pain associated with the hurt.

> *Think of it this way. When you break an arm or a leg, your body releases adrenaline, which helps you deal with the pain. After a while the pain will slowly return and be felt. At this point you are aware that there is a problem that needs to be addressed and, if not treated properly, will continue to be a source of pain for the rest of your natural life.*

It is the same for emotional pain. We get hurt and the adrenaline takes over and masks the real issue. We never deal with it because it is too painful to do so, and so we live a life of pain. Pain causes us to suffer, and when we suffer our bodies have to deal with stress, which then can lead to anxiety and depression—all of which have been already described. We have little or no desire to deal with pain, which in turn causes more problems and leads to death, literally and figuratively.

Pride

One of the biggest obstacles to overcome is pride. We think we know best; therefore, we do not seek out help. In so doing, we deny ourselves the opportunity for healing and growth. Pride is one of the biggest tools the devil uses to isolate us from help and destroy us. Pride keeps us from being humble and lets us think we have all the answers

The Purpose of Revelation

to life's problems. In biblical terms, pride does not mean simple arrogance or ostentation. Instead, it means "hubris," preferring self-will to God's will. So, pride, according to the Word of Elohim, is "every high matter that exalts itself against the knowledge of Elohim" (2 Corinthians 10:5). Pride keeps us from winning and keeps us sinning. It is the thing that gets in the way of growth, healing and deliverance and prevents us from being all that God has called us to be.

Pride keeps us from winning and keeps us sinning.

We need to understand that there is a very fine line between arrogance and confidence. We often err on the side of arrogance, thinking that we are doing Elohim a great favor. It is written:

> *"Do not love the world nor that which is in the world. If anyone loves the world, the love of the Father is not in him. Because all that is in the world – the lust of the flesh, the lust of the eyes, and the pride of life – is not of the Father but is of the world" (1 John 2:15-16).*

Resentment

Resentment (also called bitterness) is a complex, multi-layered emotion that has been described as a mixture of disappointment, disgust, anger and fear. Disappointment happens when our expectations of someone or something are not met. When we become disappointed, it is very easy to slip from disappointment to anger and then from anger to hatred. Resentment is a powerful emotion and can take root in our hearts very quickly, turning us into bitter, depressed and selfish individuals who are miserable and merciless. Resentment is one of the devil's tools we need to deal with every day—and quickly—so that it does not take root in us and destroy us. It needs to be treated like the sin it is, not just as an emotion.

Shame

Shame is defined as "a painful feeling of humiliation or distress caused by the consciousness of wrong or foolish behavior."[7] We all have indulged in some wrong or foolish behavior that could be a cause of our shame. We continue to live with this shame out of fear—fear of being humiliated publicly by the ones we love and cherish and vice versa. So, we cover up the shame and pretend that nothing is wrong. This causes even further damage, leading to feelings of utter hopelessness and eventually even physical death. Notice that shame creates in us a feeling of humiliation, not actual humiliation. Shame has a physical effect on the body as well; it destroys our immune system and takes its toll on our health. Shame is much more powerful than just being a feeling; it is a destroyer of humans. Shame is from the devil, not from God, and we need to take authority over it, see it for what it is, and root it out of our lives. We need to feel the conviction of the Spirit of Elohim to stand up to our shame and declare it as sin in our lives. Then we will start to make progress in our spiritual growth and wholeness.

> *Let my story illustrate some of what I have mentioned in the preceding paragraphs. My life has been a mix of great professional success coupled with great personal failure. One judge, whom I played golf with, described some testimonies that he had heard in his courtroom as not very useful, but very colorful. This statement could sum up my life quite easily. I had led a very colorful life, but not a very useful one, according to me and probably a host of other people, too. When I got saved in July of 1999, I was recently divorced for the third time, had resigned from the military, and was on the path to who knows where. I was not looking for Yahweh, but He found me anyway. The encounter radically changed my life. There were a few things*

---

[7] Microsoft Bing, s.v. "shame," accessed June 10, 2021, https://www.bing.com/.

that hindered my deliverance, mostly stemming from myself, because of the persistence of the devil and the fact that I was listening to what he was saying. I thought that I was never going to be good enough because of my past, and this lie stood in my way of getting to where Elohim wanted me to be. I felt shame and guilt for what I had done in my personal life. These feelings needed to be addressed as quickly as possible. Looking back, I now realize that it was pride that got in the way. I did not believe what the Word of Elohim said because I thought I had to sort it out myself. This was a lie from the devil because there is no way we can ever be good enough to handle things ourselves. But pride is the biggest sin we have because it lets us think that we know better than Yahweh, leading us to try and do things our own way, which, according to the Word of Elohim, leads to death.

What Is My Desire?
Once we have got rid of, or overcome, the obstacles we just discussed, then we are almost set to go. But there is one little thing, which is a big thing, that might be the difference between success and failure for us. It is regarding desire, and the question here is, whose desire is it? Is it mine or is it His? The simple answer is that it should be my desire to do the will of the Father in heaven (see Matthew 7:21). In other words, our desire should be to do the desire of our Father; we should be forsaking our own personal wishes and desires to fulfill His "good and well-pleasing and perfect desire" for us (Romans 12:2).

Our desire should be to do the will of our Father who is in heaven. That desire is to be sought and pursued and followed after every day. It needs to be hunted down and overtaken so that we fulfill that which is written in Scripture. We need to align our desire to the desire of Elohim and follow after Him.

This is where Romans 12 comes into play, for if we transform our minds and allow the Spirit of Elohim to lead us, then we will know these things. We will be able to prove what is the "good and well-pleasing and perfect desire of Elohim" for our lives, and we will "know that all matters work together for good to those who love Elohim, to those who are called according to his purpose" (Romans 8:28). Once again, this passage tells us that it will work out for the good to those who love Elohim … for if we "have all belief, so as to remove mountains, but do not have love, [we] are none at all" (1 Corinthians 13:2).

Chapter Seven
The Pain of Dealing

Deal

> *"Search me, O El, and know my heart; try me and know my thoughts; and see if an idolatrous way is in me, and lead me in the way everlasting" (Psalm 139:23-24).*

These verses in Psalm 139 set the tone for our dealing with our problems; it starts off with a simple statement to the very One who created us. The writer, David, states quite clearly that he has been searched by Elohim, and he is known. He continues by stating that whatever he does, it is known by Elohim; whatever he thinks is known by Elohim; whatever he is about to speak is known by Elohim. The writer carries on about not being able to flee from Elohim, then praises the Creator for how awesomely and wondrously he has been made, how he was covered in his mother's womb and "shaped in a hidden place, knit together in the depths of the earth" (verse 15). It is incredible to think about how a body is formed and shaped. There must be a plan, a blueprint, for this amazing event; there is just too much happening for it to be a coincidence. Can we even begin to understand the complexity of just this single miracle? We are "awesomely and wondrously made," verse 14 declares, and it is just that.

There is no coincidence here, for the Creator of heaven and earth who put this all together made us in His image for His good pleasure and His desire (see Ephesians 1:5). When He was creating the world and all the things in it, He spoke the word, and it happened. "Let light come to be," He commanded, and it was so (Genesis 1:3). Elohim commanded these things to happen; He spoke them into existence—is it any wonder that the power of life and death is in the tongue, according to Proverbs 18:21? (But I digress just a little.) Please note that Elohim spoke the world into existence. He commanded things to happen, and they did ... except for man. He did not say, "Let there be man"; it is written that Elohim "formed the man out of dust from the ground" (Genesis 2:7). He formed mankind; He did not just speak them. Elohim touched man with His holy hands, He formed man in His image, and then He "breathed into his nostrils breath of lives. And the man became a living being" (verse 7). This is awesome stuff. Elohim formed us, breathed the breath of life into us, and we became living beings. If this does not move you, then you need a breath of life.

The psalmist ends the psalm with the verses quoted earlier: "Search me, O El, and know my heart; try me, and know my thoughts; and see if an idolatrous way is in me, and lead me in the way everlasting." So, the very Elohim who formed us knows exactly how we are made, how we are put together, and how we function. We should ask Him then, just as David did, to search us and know our hearts, to try us and know our thoughts, and to show us any ways that need attention and need to be dealt with. Sounds simple enough, right? But we have seen the obstacles that we have to face in order to get to this part, and only once we have gotten to the end of ourselves, only once we have surrendered to Elohim and stopped giving Him orders and interfering with His work, can we truly start making forward progress and become whole and healed.

So Why Doesn't It Work?
So, we have seen that our process does not work because we do not know where to start with the problems. We, as humans, enjoy symptomatic relief of problems because it takes away the pain and gives us a false sense of

victory. Once the pain is subdued, we think the problem is over and we get on with our lives. But this is not so; the pain is only temporarily delayed until the next time. We fail to deal with the deeper issue that is causing the pain because it hurts too much or because we just don't want to deal with it. It is much like having a problem with our motor vehicle—we realize that there is a problem, but we do not know how or where to fix it.

When problems have been revealed to us, we need to take action and get the job done. And in order to get the job done, we need the right attitude (correct thinking) and the right equipment. Once the right equipment is acquired, we need to learn how to use the tools so that the right result can be achieved. For this reason, we need the full armor of Elohim.

Armor of Elohim

Stand up, "put on the complete armour of Elohim" (Ephesians 6:11), and prepare for war, for this is it. In order to go to war, we need to be prepared and ready, and that means physically, mentally and spiritually. In order to get ready, we need to change our thinking: we need to come to repentance of where we are at and where we need to be and what we need to do in order to get from where we are to where we should be. And in order to be prepared, we need to put on the equipment for warfare, just as any soldier would do when going into combat. Let's look at what the Word of Elohim has to say regarding this topic.

> *"Be strong in the Master and in the mightiness of His strength. Put on the complete armour of Elohim, for you to have power to stand against the schemes of the devil. Because we do not wrestle against flesh and blood, but against principalities, against authorities, against the world-rulers of the darkness of this age, against spiritual matters of wickedness in the heavenlies. Because of this, take up the complete armour of Elohim, so that you have power to withstand in the wicked day, and having done all, to stand" (Ephesians 6:10-13).*

Reading this, we see that we are not strong in ourselves but in the Master. If we know anything about martial arts, then we know that the master is the one who is revered as the expert in the field of his art, so in the context of this scripture, we are to be strong in Him. We are then further commanded to put on the whole armor of Elohim. Why? So we can have the power to stand against the schemes of the devil. Why is this important? If we go into battle without the proper equipment, then we are going to get hurt and possibly killed. We are to get the right equipment so we can persevere during the battle to the end. And, more importantly, is this:

> *"Because we do not wrestle against flesh and blood, but against principalities, against authorities, against the world-rulers of the darkness of this age, against spiritual matters of wickedness in the heavenlies" (Ephesians 6:12).*

This battle is a spiritual one, manifest in the flesh and fought here on earth, but still spiritual in nature. We cannot fight this battle in our own might and in our own power because we will definitely lose. We need to fight in a spiritual manner, and we do so by putting on the complete armor of Elohim. We need to examine this armor to get a better understanding of it and how to use it in our daily combat with the devil.

The good news is that the battle has already been won for us, but that does not mean we can be complacent, arrogant and lazy in our approach; if we are, then we will fall short and cause our own demise. We need to know our equipment and how to use it; otherwise it's useless and will cause no damage to the enemy in any way. Know your equipment and how to use it.

Know your equipment and how to use it.

---

1. We need to "stand, then, having *girded [our] waist with truth*" (Ephesians 6:14). *Gird* can be defined as circling the waist with a belt so that a sword or weapon can be secured to the body. What *truth* is being mentioned here? The truth is

the Word of Elohim, which is simply the self-expression of Yahweh. Yeshua says that He is "the Way, and the Truth, and the Life. No one comes to the Father except through Me" (John 14:6). This truth is the Word of Elohim, in living form.

"And the Word became flesh and pitched His tent among us, and we saw His esteem, esteem as of an only brought-forth of a father, complete in favour and truth" (John 1:14).

The great and uncomfortable thing about this truth is that it is absolute and inconvenient; it is "the same yesterday, and today, and forever" (Hebrews 13:8); and "in the beginning was the Word, and the Word was with Elohim, and the Word was Elohim" (John 1:1). This is the truth that we need around our waists; it is the encircling around us with the Word of Elohim that is a protection against everything else, against every bit of knowledge that comes "against the knowledge of Elohim" (2 Corinthians 10:5).

2. We need to *"put on the breastplate of righteousness"* (Ephesians 6:14). The breastplate is designed to protect the area where the heart is. Our hearts need protecting because we cannot be vulnerable in this area. Righteousness can be explained as the active and passive obedience to Yeshua Messiah and to the laws of Elohim. So this breastplate guards us and allows us to be obedient to the Word of Elohim.
3. We need to fit our *"feet with the preparation of the Good News of peace"* (Ephesians 6:15). This good news is the gift of Elohim to us for salvation, not by our own works, but by His alone. And why is this piece of armor on our feet? It is because the Word of Elohim "is a lamp to my feet and a light to my path" (Psalm 119:105). Without the Word of Elohim, we will stumble in the darkness and fall and perish.
4. Above all, take *"up the shield of belief* with which you shall have power to quench all the burning arrows of the wicked one"

(Ephesians 6:16). The "shield of belief" is a protection we can hide behind to avoid being destroyed by the enemy's attack. Just as Yeshua used the shield (belief in the Word) when He was tempted by the devil in the wilderness, we, too, are to use it in the same manner to protect ourselves from temptation and attacks.
5. We must *"take also the helmet of deliverance"* (Ephesians 6:17), which is there to protect our heads. This is where the thoughts and emotions are derived from, so we need to protect our thoughts from the wicked one.
6. We must take up *"the sword of the Spirit, which is the Word of Elohim"* (Ephesians 6:17). This is important, again, because the Word of Elohim is the only truth there is.

> *"For the Word of Elohim is living, and working, and sharper than any two-edged sword, cutting through even to the dividing of being and spirit, and of joints and marrow, and able to judge the thoughts and intentions of the heart" (Hebrews 4:12).*

The Word is a powerful weapon, one that can divide the spirit from the flesh. This weapon, together with the shield of belief, is the most powerful combination we have at our disposal. But we need to learn to use this weapon because, without training, we will be useless and can cause a lot of damage to ourselves and to others.

When Yeshua was tempted in the wilderness, He wielded the Word of Elohim against the wicked one by simply saying, "It is written." That phrase right there is the power of the sword of the Spirit. This passage ends with the following:

> *"Praying at all times, with all prayer and supplication [petition] in the Spirit, watching in all perseverance and supplication for all the set-apart [born again] ones" (Ephesians 6:18).*

The key elements are, firstly, that we are to put on the whole armor of Elohim; we are in battle, daily, against the schemes of the wicked one. And second, we are to learn, through training that is grounded in the Word of Elohim, so that we can "withstand in the wicked day, and having done all, to stand" (Ephesians 6:13). The rest of this book will show us how we can accomplish that. We need to be whole and complete in order to accomplish what we have been called to do. This does not necessarily mean that we are going to be qualified to do what we have been called to do; it simply means that we are called and will be made whole and complete, lacking in nothing (see James 1:4). We have been called to battle, and unless we are properly prepared and equipped, we will fail. We have been given this equipment for our own good and for victory so that we, having done all, can stand.

Repentance

> *"Bear, therefore, fruits worthy of repentance" (Matthew 3:8).*

We have not yet come to repentance of our sins as mentioned in this verse, which means that we have not changed our thinking about what this book has discussed or what is going on in our lives. We sometimes still think that we know better because we know ourselves and therefore do the things we do because we are unrepentant. To repent simply means to change the way we think about things ... so it is best that we start thinking with the mind of Yeshua.

> *"Therefore, having girded up the loins of your mind, being sober, set your expectation perfectly upon the favour that is to be brought to you at the revelation of Yeshua Messiah, as obedient children, not conforming yourselves to the former lusts in your ignorance" (1 Peter 1:13-14).*

We need to walk in repentance, meaning that it is not just a "once and done" thing but a constant, daily walk in the renewing of our minds. We need to have the full armor of Elohim on so that we can live victoriously, day after day. We need to bear fruits worthy of repentance, meaning that our actions will show and communicate that we have changed the way we think. Actions speak louder than words.

Courage

"For Elohim has not given us a spirit of cowardice, but of power and of love and of self-control" (2 Timothy 1:7).

The first step in the process of dealing with issues is courage. We need courage to begin a task that may seem overwhelming or daunting to us, especially when pain and painful memories are involved. We, as humans, tend to shy away from pain because it is an unpleasant experience for most of us. There can be no pleasure in being emotionally hurt through a bad and abusive relationship; there can no pleasure in being so distraught and downcast that ending our life seems like the best and only option. So, in order to proceed with the dealing part, we need courage. The good news is that we have been given that courage already; we just need to use it. Like the muscles which we all have, we need to exercise them if they are to grow and be healthy and of good use. But, that is easier said than done, simply because we don't have a firm belief in Elohim and in His written Word. The Word of Elohim says here that we have not been given "a spirit of cowardice, but of power and of love and of self-control." Think about this for a moment. We have not been given a spirit of cowardice; rather, we have been blessed with a spirit of power, love, and self-control. And if we believe this to be true, then why are we so afraid? What are we afraid of?

"There is no fear in love, but perfect love casts out fear, because fear holds punishment, and he who fears has not been made perfect in love" (1 John 4:18).

This means that even though we are far from perfect, we have the wonderful blessing of this spirit that must be used for the purpose it was intended.

As with muscles, when they are not used, they atrophy. In other words, they waste away, usually because of a lack of physical activity.

(There are times when this atrophy happens as a result of disease or illness, but I want to deal with the atrophy due to lack of use.)

Often times we have spiritual atrophy because we fail to use the gift that has been given to us and are overcome by fear, which kills us more than death itself.

> *I am reminded of a story I once heard of a baby in a day care center that was suffering from malnutrition and had every kind of allergy imaginable. The baby was not healthy and was not as developed, in speech and movement, as the other babies of its age. When the day care owner, who is a godly woman, asked the parent what was happening, what was the baby eating, the mother replied that the child was only on milk formula. The Spirit of Elohim prompted the day care owner to start feeding the baby regular food, and within a few days the baby started responding. Soon the allergies were gone, and the baby started developing normally. This is because at the age of six months, babies should be given solid foods to support and promote, not only physical growth, but also mental development.*

This situation is much like a verse in Hebrews chapter 5. Here the writer is talking to the Christians about the priesthood in the Christian faith. The first eleven verses are quite inspiring, to say the least, but in verse 12 he rebukes the people by saying that by this time they ought to be teachers of the Word, but instead they still need someone to teach them the first elements, the basic elements, of the words of Elohim. Because they were not eating solid food, they had spiritually atrophied to the point of milk again; they had become stunted and even regressive in their growth.

> **"For everyone partaking of milk is inexperienced in the word of righteousness, for he is a babe" (Hebrews 5:13).**

In other words, when we are on milk and not on solid foods, we have no understanding of righteousness.

This is a powerful statement as it shows our weakness when we have not used the gift of the Spirit given to us. The writer goes on further to say that solid food is for the mature, for those whose senses have been *trained* by practice to discern both good and evil. Let us understand a few things here. When we are babies on milk, we are not mature and have no understanding of righteousness. When we are mature disciples, we are on solid food and our senses have been trained by practice to discern between good and evil. We are expected to train by practice … this does not happen by itself.

We are expected to train by practice.

So, coming back to the spirit of fear and atrophy, we have become lame and weak and immature because we have not exercised, by practice, the spirit of self-control given to us. We need to take heed here and ensure that we practice self-control every day. If we practice, then we exercise our gift and giftings, become mature in our stature, and "grow in the favour and knowledge of our Master and Saviour יהושע Messiah" (2 Peter 3:18).

We need to exercise the spirit of power given to us; we need to exercise the spirit of love and of self-control. First, though, we need to believe that this is indeed the truth. If you doubt this, then go back to the section on belief and re-read it. We need to believe that Elohim "is, and that He is a rewarder of those who earnestly seek Him" (Hebrews 11:6).

Ask

"Ask and it shall be given to you, seek and you shall find, knock and it shall be opened to you" (Matthew 7:7).

We are commanded to seek and knock. Thus, the second step in this process is to ask. We don't, for a number of reasons. One is that we might not like the answer we get; another is that we are afraid of the outcome. In other words, we might receive an answer that does not suit our narrative and does not fit into our mold; we fear that we might have to do something with the answer that we don't want to be responsible for. Other possible reasons are that we are arrogant and full of pride, thinking we can solve it on our own, or because we know we are guilty and just have no desire to deal with the problem, hoping it will disappear on its own. Whatever the reason, we need to ask if we want to make any progress on this journey.

In the story of the thief on the cross in Luke 23:39-41, the first thief is hanging next to Yeshua, and the second thief tells Yeshua that if He is indeed the Messiah, then why does He not save Himself and the two thieves? The first thief then turns to the second thief and reminds him sternly that they are hanging there because they deserve to, but Yeshua has done nothing wrong. You see, the thief acknowledged his wrongdoing and that he deserved to be crucified. He accepted responsibility for his actions.

Too often in life we want to blame others for our downfall and for our woes and troubles. We want others to fix our problems for us without our doing anything. We want everyone else to be responsible for us; we don't want to be the cause of our infirmities. It is easy to say "the devil made me do it" or "you made me angry" or "it's because of you that I am where I am today." The thief who took responsibility for his actions then asked Yeshua to remember him when He came into His reign. Yeshua answered him, "Truly, I say to you today, you shall be with Me in paradise" (Luke 23:43). When we take responsibility for our actions and deeds, we start from a position of strength, and how we see that position is purely a matter of attitude and determination.

> *I am reminded of a real story mentioned in a conversation of twin brothers who grew up in despicable conditions in their home; they were taken from their parents and placed in foster care. When they were of age, they went on about their business. A few years went by, and the foster care agency decided to track them down to find out how they were*

> *doing. The one brother was married, had a great family, had a great job and was doing really well. When they asked him why, he replied, "If you knew how I grew up and what I went through, then you would understand why." The agency tracked down the second brother and found him living under a tree, a homeless alcoholic and drug-addicted bum. They asked him why, to which he responded, "If you knew how I grew up and what I went through, then you would understand why."*

Accepting responsibility is the key when we ask.

Philippians 4:6-7 spells out clearly that we are to be anxious of nothing:

> **"Do not worry at all, but in every matter, by prayer and petition, with thanksgiving, let your requests be made known to Elohim and the peace of Elohim, which surpasses all understanding, shall guard your hearts and minds through Messiah יהושע."**

We need to spend some time studying this passage so that we can properly dissect it and understand the very essence of what is being said.

1. *"Do not worry at all."* We are commanded here not to worry, but we are disobedient and do. We counter the very command given and then wonder why we are in ill health. Worrying leads to anxiety, which causes a rise in cortisol in our bodies. When that happens, our immune systems are depleted and our health starts failing. Apart from that, anxiety can lead to other terrible addictions and lifestyle choices that are harmful and eventually lead to our death. Remember, the aim of the thief is to come and "to steal, and to slaughter, and to destroy" ... but He has "come that [we] might possess life, and that [we]

might possess it beyond measure" (John 10:10). So, worry leads to anxiety and anxiety leads to death. Here are those life and death choices again. "Do not worry at all." Life and death choices ....
2. *"By prayer and petition."* What does this phrase mean? Prayer is rather self-explanatory, keeping in mind that we need to talk directly with Elohim, not through meditation or contemplation, but directly with Him. The second part, petition, is a formal request or plea to Elohim that pertains to a certain cause or problem. By definition, a plea is a formal request to Elohim to take action, or to make a ruling, on a certain issue or case.[1] For example, if you tithed faithfully but have not seen a blessing as promised in the Word of Elohim, you could then petition Yahweh to hear your case and ask for Him to make a decision on your behalf. Yeshua intercedes on our behalf; in other words, He is like a lawyer representing you in a big court case before the supreme Judge of the universe. Our petitions are the formal requests while our prayers are regular communication with Yahweh.
3. *"With thanksgiving."* What does this phrase mean? It means having a thankful attitude, as in "count it all joy when you fall into various trials" (James 1:2). It is *praise to Elohim*. In the Word of Elohim, thanksgiving reflected adoration, sacrifice, praise or an offering. Thanksgiving was a grateful expression to Elohim as an act of worship. Rarely, if ever, was thanksgiving extended to any person or thing, except Elohim.

Wow, how I have fallen short of including thanksgiving too many times to mention. I am reminded of a story of a man who is in the ministry and has been blessed beyond measure with everything he could ever need. One evening he was preaching at

---

[1] Microsoft Bing, s.v. "plea," accessed June 11, 2021, https://www.bing.com/.

a church when the power of the Spirit of Elohim began moving powerfully, to the extent that one woman who needed money was given a blank check by another person and told to fill in the amount, another was blessed with a car, and so it went. At the end of the evening when he was leaving, he was given an envelope. On the ride home he opened it to find a check for five hundred dollars. Being tired, he thought he might have missed a zero on the check and stopped to put the light on so that he could make sure. But no, there was no extra zero, only the five hundred dollars. He was really disappointed and started mumbling about it to Elohim. Elohim then asked him what it was that he needed. Did he need money for his house? The answer was no. Did he need money for his kids' school? The answer was no. The questions went on for a while, and each question was answered with a no. Then Elohim told him that according to His reckoning then, he had five hundred dollars to spend on whatever he wanted. Elohim further instructed him to get out of the car and jump for joy. I wish you could have seen the demonstration that was given to me because it was the funniest thing I had seen in a while. But picture a man with a very unimpressed look on his face, trying to jump for joy when there was none. It is like sitting in the corner when scolded, but still standing up on the inside. It was a clear case of lack of thanksgiving. The end of the story is that this man was able to jump for joy, as Elohim had commanded him, and he enjoyed the five hundred dollars, with thanksgiving.

4. *"Let your requests be made known to Elohim."* Only at this point do we get to make our requests known. Once each of the conditions already discussed are met, then

The Pain of Dealing

we are to make our requests known. I often cringe when people pray because they treat Elohim like a servant, like a heavenly butler. "Do this, do that" ... no request is being made; instead, we are barking orders at the Almighty Elohim. It is disrespectful. We should never wonder why our prayers are not being heard or met. Elohim does not take orders from us, and we need to understand this truth very clearly.

If you want to study more about prayer, read Matthew 6. There Yeshua Himself said how we ought to pray. If you read from the beginning of the chapter, you will see that He sets up the way we ought to pray very well. We would do well to heed this instruction if we want our prayers heard and answered.

So now that we have followed the conditions set for us in Philippians, what happens then? The very next verse in Philippians says this:

"And the peace of Elohim, which surpasses all understanding, shall guard your hearts and minds through Messiah Yeshua" (Philippians 4:7).

You see, once we have met all the criteria for praying, once we have been obedient to the commands of Yeshua, then the end result is this peace, this wonderful peace that passes all of our human understanding.

When I was freshly saved, I was gainfully unemployed, meaning that I was okay not to have a job for a short period of time, by my own choice. I knew that I would need to get a job soon because I needed to pay bills and live, etc., but I had been invited on a mission trip to Mozambique with a group of American and Canadian people. I was torn between going on the mission or finding a job, so I petitioned Elohim on this matter. I had a thankful heart, I was not anxious,

> *but I needed clarity on what to do. The answer was crystal clear: I was to go on the mission trip, which led to several other amazing things happening to me. The peace that I felt about going and not getting a job was beyond human comprehension. I had no anxiety about a job or about the bills I had to pay; I had tremendous peace, that peace written of in Philippians. This is what happens when we are obedient to the Word of Elohim; He will never leave us or forsake us (see Hebrews 13:5). His Word is the only truth there is; it is the same yesterday, today and for evermore (see Hebrews 13:8).*

In summary, then, come before Elohim with no anxiety, with thanksgiving in your heart, and make your requests known to Elohim. Ask the Creator, the very One who created you, to search you and know your heart. Ask Him to try you and know your thoughts to see if there is any idolatrous way in you, and ask Him to lead you in the everlasting way. Then you can courageously ask, and you will experience peace, the peace that surpasses all understanding, that will guard your hearts and minds through Messiah Yeshua. (See Psalm 139:23-24; Philippians 4:6-7.)

Obedience

> ***"If you love Me, you shall guard My commands" (John 14:15).***

This is quite an opening statement. What if the commands are hard to follow? What if Yeshua does not understand what we are going through? What if we think we know ourselves better than anyone else? Then we are free from following the commands, right? No, wrong! We have already established from Psalm 139 that Elohim has searched us and knows us and that He formed us in the depths of the earth. Why then are we still doubting this? If we say we believe—and "belief is the substance of what we expect, the proof of what is not seen" (Hebrews 11:1)—then why are we reluctant to do what has been commanded of us? There is one overwhelming reason: we don't love Yeshua the way we ought to. Because we don't have this love, we are disobedient. It is clearly written that if we love Him, we will "guard" or obey His commands

I don't want to belabor the point, but we need to have the firmest grasp of love and know its power and purpose. If you are still struggling with this topic, then I suggest you go back and read the section on love again before moving on. Remember, the basis of this whole journey is love.

> *"And now belief, expectation [hope], and love remain – these three. But the greatest of these is love" (1 Corinthians 13:13).*

This is a great statement to make, and we should understand the context of it here so that we can follow the commands and be obedient.

This love, which compelled Yeshua to die on the cross for you and me, is so strong that it will let us die for our friends.

> *"No one has greater love than this: that one should lay down his life for his friends" (John 15:13).*

What exactly does it mean to lay down your life? It means that you willingly and selflessly sacrifice your own life for others. Your life is not taken from you; you give it.

> *I am reminded of the film The Last Samurai, where the head of the samurai goes to the emperor, whom he is serving, and falls flat on his face before his ruler and says, "If you want my life, you don't have to take it. Tell me, and I will give it to you gladly." What makes this so special is that, in the context of the film, the emperor was wanting to do away with*

> *the samurai, having them killed, and yet the leader was willing to give his life instead of it being taken.*[2]

This story pales into insignificance when compared to Yeshua, who laid down His life for us. He willingly gave His life for us; He sacrificed His life and laid it down for us so that we might be saved. This is the love we need to have—this powerful and moving love that compels us to live a life of obedience to the very One who gave His life for us.

We need the love that compels us to a life of obedience.

So then, why are we disobedient? It is because we do not have enough love. Period. Much like patience, love is a fruit of the Spirit of Elohim (see Galatians 5:22), and if we don't have it, it is because we have not tended to and nurtured this fruit. We became depleted of love and failed to renew it daily. I think we believe that love is there, or it is not. We think it is like fuel in a car: it is there, or it is not. But, like fuel, it needs to be replenished. When you use the vehicle, it consumes fuel and will eventually run out when not refueled. This happens to us, too; we run out of this fuel called love because we don't replenish it from the very Source, the Spirit of Elohim. Yeshua Himself did refuel regularly. We read of Him going away from everyone to be quiet and to replenish His fruit (see Mark 1:35, for example).

I also believe we disobey because we think we know better. We think we know how to fix things better than the Creator Himself. We think we can figure it out for ourselves. This is known as pride or arrogance, which is defined as a feeling of superiority and having an inflated self-esteem.[3] There is nothing wrong with having self-esteem; it is a unique feature of our created being. It is when this self-esteem

---

[2] "Katsomoto and Emperor sword scene," *The Last Samurai*, directed by Edward Zwick (USA: Warner Brothers, December 2003), DVD.
[3] *Merriam-Webster.com Dictionary*, s.v. "arrogance," accessed June 11, 2021, https://www.merriam-webster.com/dictionary/arrogance.

takes over and we feel superior that it becomes a problem. The first sin ever committed was by the devil himself, which resulted in him being kicked out of heaven (see Isaiah 14:12). The devil wanted to be as high as Elohim; he was arrogant, and when pride entered his heart, he fell. Proverbs states it clearly when it says that "before destruction comes pride, and before a fall a haughty spirit" (Proverbs 16:18). If you don't know what haughty means, here is a quick definition as well as a list of synonyms for us to ponder: "arrogantly superior and disdainful...proud, vain, arrogant, conceited, snobbish, stuck-up, pompous, self-important, superior, egotistical, supercilious, condescending, lofty, patronizing, smug, scornful, contemptuous, disdainful, overweening, overbearing, imperious, lordly, cavalier."[4]

We can see that being haughty is really not a good thing. As a matter of fact, it is sinful. It is a lie from the very pit of hell because it makes us think more highly of ourselves than we should. We need to stand against it and the stronghold it represents.

The Word of Elohim says:

> ***"For the weapons we fight with are not fleshly but mighty in Elohim for overthrowing strongholds, overthrowing reasonings and every high matter that exalts itself against the knowledge of Elohim, taking captive every thought to make it obedient to the Messiah, and being ready to punish all disobedience, when your obedience is complete" (2 Corinthians 10:4-6).***

The Word of Elohim also shares how the Messiah, after spending forty days and nights in the wilderness, comes out and is tempted (tried) by the devil. (Read Matthew 4:1-11.) The devil says to Yeshua that if He is the Son of Elohim, then He should command the stones to be turned to bread. Now, this is a reasonable thing to say because Yeshua was, is and will forever be the Son of Elohim. He could have done that, given that He was hungry. But Yeshua is obedient; He takes every thought captive and simply says, "It is written ...." He could

---

4 Microsoft Bing, s.v. "haughty," accessed June 11, 2021, https://www.bing.com/.

have had a discourse with the devil and tried to reason why or tried to explain, but He knew what real authority was and where it came from and used that authority to answer. We often try to reason and justify our thinking and reasoning with sound arguments, but we become prideful and arrogant and set them up against the knowledge of Elohim. Once again, we need to believe that the Word of Elohim is the truth. When we do, we know that every time we follow our own way, we become arrogant and full of pride.

> *I once attended a talk given by a university professor who claimed to be a leading expert on the subject of emotional intelligence. Having read the book by Daniel Goleman[5], I thought the professor's claim was rather pretentious, but listened to what the man had to say. At one point during his talk, he mentioned that a sign of emotional intelligence is independent thought. This got me thinking of the scripture in John 5:19 where Yeshua tells the people that He, the Son, can do nothing of His own but that which He sees the Father doing. The world will lead you to believe that independent thought is a sign of intelligence and that we need to use it, but I am wary of this thinking because it leads to pride and arrogance, and we use knowledge to puff ourselves up against the knowledge of Elohim (see 1 Corinthians 8:1).*

The story of Saul in 1 Samuel 15 is quite relevant here. Samuel is sent to Saul to give him a message from Elohim. The message is to form an army and go attack the Amalekites and destroy them. He is to kill everything in sight—all the people, the livestock—everything. Saul does as he is told and attacks the enemy, killing everyone and everything except the enemy king, whom he takes captive, and the best of the fattened calves, oxen and sheep. Clearly he was not obedient here. In his own mind sparing these animals was the right thing to do, for he could use one of the animals to sacrifice to Elohim as a praise offering. Great idea? Not so much.

---

[5] Daniel Goleman, *Emotional Intelligence: Why It Can Matter More Than IQ* (New York: Bantam Books, 1995).

The Pain of Dealing

Elohim says, in effect, "I regret that I made Saul king." Wow, that is quite a statement. When Samuel confronts Saul, there is a discourse between the two men where Saul tries to rationalize these actions and blame his people for taking the sheep and the cattle.

> *"Then Shemu'el said, 'Does יהוה delight in ascending offerings and slaughterings [sacrifices], as in obeying the voice of יהוה? Look, to obey is better than a slaughtering, to heed is better than the fat of rams. For rebellion is as the sin of divination, and stubbornness is as wickedness and idolatry. Because you have rejected the word of יהוה , He also does reject you as sovereign'" (1 Samuel 15:22-23).*

This is hard to read, but simply put, obedience is better than sacrifice, in every area of our lives. We need to be obedient to Elohim instead of sacrificing things that we think are important.

We need to listen to Elohim, as doing so is better than offering the fat of rams. Obedience is the key here—listening and doing what we are told to do. Samuel goes on to say that rebellion, of which disobedience is a part, is like the sin of divination, which is defined as the art of consulting supernatural powers in order to be able to foretell the future.[6] So, when we rebel against the Word of Elohim, we are sinning, and we can see here that rebellion is evil. So is disobedience. Therefore, we need to get rid of disobedience, realizing that disobedience could be part of the problem holding us back from being whole.

Obedience is better than sacrifice, in every area of our lives.

Obedience is a by-product of love; it is not the product itself. Therefore, we need to focus on love and know that obedience will happen if

---

6 Microsoft Bing, s.v. "divination," accessed June 11, 2021, https://www.bing.com/.

we do so. Too often we focus on the end result instead of on the process and so get sidetracked. The Word of Elohim is very clear on this matter, that obedience is driven by love, not fear, as it is written:

> *"And this is the love, that we walk according to His commands. This is the command, that as you have heard from the beginning, you should walk in it" (2 John 1:6).*

To confirm this truth even more, we can take this walking just a step further to where we are commanded not only to walk according to the commands, but also to guard them. The Word says:

> *"If you guard My commands, you shall stay in My love even as I have guarded My Father's commands and stay in His love" (John 15:10).*

So, let's state this clearly. We decide to be obedient, which is a life choice, and that decision brings blessings to us. We decide to obey because of love, not sacrifice or fear. It is a choice we make because "we love Him because He first loved us" and "He laid down His life for us" (1 John 3:16; 4:19). We walk according to His commands and guard His commands, which leads to obedience, and we do all this not out of fear but in love.

Path

There is a path to be followed when we go on this journey, and it is not an easy one, although it is a necessary one. Walking this path is not going to be a breeze, but we have everything we need for this trip through the Spirit of Elohim. This path is described in the following section, and we need to "embrace the suck," as they would say in the military. Walking this path is going to suck, but it is what it is, and we need to embrace it with everything we have.

> *"And not only this, but we also exult in pressures, knowing that pressure works endurance; and*

endurance, approvedness; and approvedness, expectation" (Romans 5:3-4).

"Not only so, but we also glory in our sufferings, because we know that suffering produces perseverance; perseverance, character; and character, hope" (Romans 5:3-4, NIV).

Suffering

"My brothers, count it all joy when you fall into various trials, knowing that the proving of your belief works endurance. And let endurance have a perfect work, so that you be perfect and complete, lacking in naught" (James 1:2-4).

We don't like suffering. I get it. But suffering is, unfortunately, a very important part of this process.

Suffering is required so that healing may take its course. I am sure that most of you have received some kind of injury in your life that resulted in pain and suffering. It is not pleasant, but when endured, the results are fantastic: there is healing and the ability to return to your usual lifestyle. If you break a bone, it eventually will heal on its own because of the great miracle of your body's working. Sometimes, though, the bone needs to be set in its proper place, and that is a painful thing because it hurts. But if that setting is not done, the bone will grow back skewed and continue to hurt for the rest of your life—unless it is reset later and returned to the right place. So it is with us. We are broken, we need fixing, we need to be set, or reset, and doing so will require pain and suffering, but only for a while. Interestingly, though, the spot where a bone has healed is stronger than it was before the break. This knowledge should encourage us in the broken areas of our lives, for when they are healed, they will be stronger than before.

The question is, do you want pain for a short while or for the rest of your life? If someone offered you pain for a day or for the rest of your life, which would you choose? If it was pain for a week or for the rest of your life, which would you pick? I think we become very shortsighted in these matters and endure painful lives because we don't want to deal with the agony of suffering for a short while. We lose sight of, or have never had sight of, the goal set for us: the goal of living life and living it in abundance (see John 10:10). Didn't that promise mean that we would have pain-free lives? Not at all. Rather, it means that we will be empowered from on high and equipped with everything "we need for life and reverence, through the knowledge of Him who called us to esteem and uprightness [righteousness]" (2 Peter 1:3).

Yeshua said:

> *"These words I have spoken to you, that in Me you might have peace. In the world you have pressure [tribulation], but take courage, I have overcome the world" (John 16:33).*

We are told in the Word that we will have tribulation in this world. We are told that we will suffer trials of many kinds, but we also are told that there is a way to deal with it, a way in which we are able to make it through, with the help of Yeshua and the Spirit of Elohim.

> *"No trial has overtaken you except such as is common to man, and Elohim is trustworthy, who shall not allow you to be tried beyond what you are able, but with the trial shall also make the way of escape, enabling you to bear it" (1 Corinthians 10:13).*

As we can see from this verse, nothing we are dealing with in life is unique—it is common to us all. Some of us deal with different things differently, but we all deal with things. Thankfully, we will never be tested beyond what we can handle. Think of being locked in a prison cell. You may not be released from the cell, but you will find freedom within its walls. First Corinthians 10:13 is a powerful scripture, and we have to believe that it is true. It does not matter what we are going through because we are not alone, we are not unique; all of it is common to the human race. All that differs is the topic—the issue remains the same.

We often only focus on the topic while greatly ignoring the issue. Dealing with the topic can be frustrating, annoying or irritating at best, while dealing with the issue becomes a painful and real experience. It is like putting a little bandage on a cancerous sore and hoping that it will go away, except all we are doing is covering up the problem and not dealing with it. We, as humans, enjoy symptomatic relief rather than dealing with the real cause. It is easier and less painful to do so. We want the pains of life to be taken away from us rather than deal with what causes the pain. We should be more like Yeshua in the garden of Gethsemane where He asks the Father, "If it is possible, let this cup pass from Me. Yet not as I desire, but as You desire" (Matthew 26:39).

All that differs is the topic—the issue remains the same.

Once we have asked Elohim to search us and know us and we have had revelation of what is required, we need to have the courage and the obedience to do something about the revelation. This is where the suffering really starts because addressing an issue is painful. It hurts to confront or deal with the things that hurt us. We also will encounter suffering at this point because we might feel justified in our feelings. We might feel that we are right to be offended by what happened to us. But we are wrong to harbor unforgiveness.

So why are we to suffer? Why can't Yeshua just take away our pain and be done with it? Well, He can, and He does, as He desires. It is not our calling to decide. More often than not, we need to suffer so that we can learn and grow.

We have read in James 1 that our suffering leads to endurance. It is important that we endure so that we can be made perfect and complete, lacking in nothing. Once again, our firm belief in the written Word is required here. If it says that we must "count it all joy" when we suffer trials of many kinds, then we need to "count it all joy" when we suffer various trials!

Why is joy so important here? How can we count it as joy when we suffer? We need to understand the importance of joy in this process because without it we are going to fail again and again. It is written that "the joy of Elohim is our strength" (Nehemiah 8:10)—the *joy* of Elohim, not His power or His love but His joy. Is it any wonder, then, that one of the fruits of the Spirit of Elohim is joy? (See Galatians 5:22.) Joy does not just happen; it is a result of a process of being filled and renewed by the Spirit of Elohim until we are full of the fruits set forth in Galatians 5.

Joy is a fruit that, when tended and nurtured and watered and looked after, will grow and produce good fruit in season. It is not a by-product of our neglect and disobedience and lawlessness; neither is it a gift to be received. So, when we have joy, we have strength. When we have strength, we can endure and are able to persevere. So how do we go about getting joy in the midst of all this pain? The Word says that those who wait on Elohim will have their strength renewed:

> ***"He gives power to the faint, and to those who have no might He increases strength. Even youths shall faint and be weary, and young men stumble and fall, but those who wait on Elohim renew their strength, they raise up the wings like eagles, they run and are not weary, they walk and do not faint" (Isaiah 40:29-31).***

In order to endure trials, we need to have strength and joy. We need the fruit of joy, which is a result of walking in the Spirit. When we walk in the Spirit, the result is an increase in the fruits of the Spirit of Elohim. So, at this point we know that we need to believe in Him who has come to set us free; we need to be obedient to the Spirit of Elohim and follow His leading so that we may obtain freedom from whatever ails us.

Think of Luke's story of Yeshua the night before He was arrested and crucified. Yeshua is on the mount of Olives and goes to pray alone. He instructs the disciples to pray so that they do not "enter into trial"; He doesn't tell them to pray for Him. He walks off a little way and falls to His knees, where He prays and asks His Father, "If it be Your counsel, remove this cup from Me. Yet not My desire, but let Yours be done" (Luke 22:42). The passage continues on to say that a messenger from heaven appeared to Him to strengthen Him, not comfort Him. Furthermore, it says that He was in agony and the sweat fell from Him "like great drops of blood falling down to the ground" (Luke 22:44). Clearly He was in agony and suffering a great deal. He knew what was coming; He knew it was going to be a day of great suffering for Him. According to Matthew's Gospel in chapter 26, He steps away a second time and prays again. He asks His Father if there is another way in which this could be done, indicating that He was willing to explore other options for you and me to have salvation. Once again, not His will but the desire of the Father was to be done.

It would be impossible to explain the anguish and the agony that Yeshua was going through that night, but I am pretty sure it was intense and painful. I am convinced that it was the most difficult thing that He ever had to do—that He willingly, meaning that He had made the choice, went to the cross for us so that we may have life, and have it in abundance.

Watching the 2004 movie *The Passion of the Christ*, directed by Mel Gibson, will definitely help you with a visual representation of the pain and suffering that the Messiah went through for us. If we are bold and courageous enough, we will not mind enduring and suffering the little bit of pain that we have, to receive healing. We have not yet sweated drops like blood falling to the ground, and we have definitely not yet given our lives, so painfully, so that others may live.

My encouragement for you today is to count it "pure joy" when you suffer "trials of many kinds, because you know that" your suffering will lead to perseverance, your perseverance will lead to character, and your character will lead to hope. (See James 1:2-3; Romans 5:3-4 NIV.) I will sum it up with one scripture here:

"Though being a Son, He learned obedience by what He suffered" (Hebrews 5:8).

The Messiah, Yeshua Himself, even though He was the Son of the most high Elohim, had to learn obedience through what He suffered. Why should we be any different to Him? Why should it be easier for us when the perfect example has been set for us?

Perseverance

> ***"Being empowered with all power, according to the might of His esteem, for all endurance and patience with joy" (Colossians 1:11).***

By this stage we should have a firm grasp on where we are on this path. We have gotten to the point of belief, we have asked and we have been obedient to the prompting of the Spirit of Elohim who has led us into all truth. The next part of the process is the perseverance part.

Notice in Colossians 1:11 it says that we are "being empowered with *all* power, according to the might of His esteem." So, why have we been "empowered with all power, according to the might of His esteem"? It is "for all endurance and patience." That means that we have the strength and power of Him, Yeshua Messiah, to be able to endure and to stand above all until the task is done.

We often give up because we have no perseverance and because we have no clear goal. We fail to see the end result. Remember what belief is? According to Hebrews 11:1, it is "the substance of what is expected, the proof of what is not seen." We fail to have real substance in our expectations and fail to see what is yet to be done. We lack the vision. We fail to see the end result or what the end result will look like.

> *I have seen lack of perseverance many times in Special Forces training. Young men come in to try and attain what few men can ever do. Most of the men are fit and able to complete the training, but most fail in their quest because of a few things. One of the biggest reasons is that they lack the perseverance to push through till the end; they quit when it gets*

> hard and tough. It is easy to keep going when things are going your way, but it is a lot harder when the odds seem stacked against you. So, when it is dark and lonely, your feet hurt, you are tired and weary, and you are hungry and cold and miserable, when things get hard, you will most likely quit if you are not properly prepared for the battle. The full armor of Elohim is your equipment in this time; use it continuously and daily in your battle to be whole.

Persevering takes courage and effort because there is no one who is going to help you along, pick you up and encourage you to keep going. The same is almost true here, except we have been given the power from on high, the same power that raised Yeshua from the dead (see Romans 8:11). This power keeps us going and keeps us moving in the right direction. We need to be empowered with all the power of His esteem, for all patience and endurance with joy. We need to keep our eyes on the prize.

We also need patience, something that we lack in most areas of our lives. I, for one, can be the most patient person when it to comes to teaching others, but put me behind the wheel of a car, and I am the worst. This means I lack patience; I do not have the fruit of the Spirit of Elohim in abundance. It is something I need to grow and develop in my own life. So, sadly, we often lack the patience to endure and persevere. The transliteration that I am quoting uses the word *perseverance* for patience, and it is interesting to note that one of the Greek words for patience is *hupômône* , which means "steadfastness in difficult circumstances." [7] We need to be steadfast in all things.

There are a number of alternative words for steadfast that might inspire you. They are abiding, changeless, faithful, dedicated, dependable, enduring, reliable, true, constant, staunch, firm, resolute, relentless, single-minded, unwavering, unfaltering, unswerving, unyielding, unflinching, inflexible and immovable.[8]

---

7 John Nel, "The Fruit of the Holy Spirit: 4 Patience," Bible Research (blog), December 12, 2016, https://johnnel.com/2016/12/12/4-patience/.
8 *Roget's 21st Century Thesaurus*, 3rd ed., s.v. "steadfast," accessed June 15, 2021, https://www.thesaurus.com/browse/steadfast.

The one word that really speaks to me is *single-mindedness*. We are to be single-minded about what we are doing; or in other words, we are to be focused on one thing. We often are distracted by the many different things that need our attention, so we become overwhelmed, anxious and impatient when trying to get things done. It is a classic case of "divide and conquer." When we are single-minded, we can focus on the given task and get it done efficiently and effectively.

> *In the military, there is a concept of war that is called the Focus of Main Effort. In other words, focus your efforts on achieving the mission; don't get sidetracked by little interferences and battles that will wear you down and beat you up before you have even reached your goal. They should not be ignored, but your focus should be on achieving the goal set before you. Too often we become involved in the little things and forget all about the main prize, and we grow so weary from the small battles that we lose the war.*

Be single-minded, be focused on the one thing that you need to do, and do it until you are finished and successful.

In the first few verses of James 1, the writer talks of perseverance and of asking for wisdom, in belief. He continues on to say that if anyone asks, that one should believe and not doubt because whoever "doubts is like a wave of the sea driven and tossed by the wind" (verse 6). He further comments two verses later that if we doubt, we are "double-minded" and "unstable" in all our ways. This is interesting because being *makrothumia*, or steadfast, means that we are single-minded. And when we are single-minded, we will be stable in all our ways. So, being single-minded is a requirement for perseverance. We need to focus on the goal set before us, being determined to reach it no matter the circumstances. We need to believe and not have doubt.

> ***"For whatever was written before was for our instruction, that through endurance and encouragement of the Scriptures we might have the expectation" (Romans 15:4).***

This is the hope that was written of in Hebrews 11, of the things we have not yet seen.

Furthermore, Romans 15:5 says:

"And the Elohim of endurance and encouragement give you to be of the same mind toward one another, according to Messiah יהושע."

This is where our perseverance comes from. It comes from "the Elohim of endurance and encouragement." It comes from the very One who loves us unfailingly, to the point of giving His life for us. It comes from the very source of love and patience that we have access to through the power of the Spirit of Elohim. None of this comes from us, but we do need to have the expectation that we can accomplish these things through the power and the might of Elohim and His Spirit. We "are more than overcomers," it is written, "through Him who loved us" (Romans 8:37). And we "have strength to do all, through Messiah who empowers" us (Philippians 4:13). We just have to believe ... and do.

Character

> *Many years ago, I had the great pleasure of meeting up with a man who has since then become a really good friend. He is an avid collector of military memorabilia, especially South African Special Forces stuff, which is quite collectible and very valuable. He had an impressive collection already and was offered the opportunity to buy a tunic, complete with medals and badges, from another collector. He did this at a huge cost to himself, then started doing some research into the history of the owner. He found out that the tunic had been stolen from the original owner and, once again, at great cost to himself, he tracked*

> *down the owner of the item and returned it. This spoke volumes to me about the character of the man because he understood the value of the item and what it cost to have earned it. Even though he had legally bought the item, he returned the stolen goods. This is a great example of character. It is about doing the right thing, even though it is not expected or even required.*

This section deals with character, and it is difficult enough to define, let alone describe. But when we are filled with the Spirit of Elohim, we will display a very different nature to the one we had before. Our character will have changed, and it will be evident for all to see. I know what I was like before I came to repentance, and I know what I am like now. Sure, there are still remnants of the old me because I often lack self-control and allow myself to get carried away by the old me, but I am a changed man, and definitely for the better. The nature of the character we need to display is spelled out for us in the following scripture:

> **"But the fruit of the Spirit is love, joy, peace, patience, kindness, goodness, trustworthiness, gentleness, self-control. Against such there is no Torah" (Galatians 5:22-23).**

By now we understand that we need to suffer because it is the beginning of a wonderful process of healing and restoration. We also know that we have been given the tools to be able to suffer—and that tool is joy, the very joy from the Spirit of Elohim living in us and on us. We have learned that our suffering will lead to perseverance because, when we persevere, we will be able to finish the work that was set for us and that we are called to do. We also know that we have been equipped to persevere by the Spirit of Elohim and that we cannot reach the goal in our own strength. All of this is fueled by love and the desire to live an abundant life in Yeshua Messiah who first loved us. So, all of these things are driven by love. As we continue with this process, it is written, our suffering will lead to perseverance and our perseverance will lead to character. Now we need to understand what this character is and why it is important to us to have.

Character is preceded by perseverance and suffering.

What is character? It is defined in the world as the "moral excellence and firmness"[9] of an individual and is made up of certain components or traits. One can be said to be a person of character if one is honest, decent or has good qualities or beliefs in life and acts according to them. But what does the Word say character is and why it is important?

> *"By their fruits you shall know them ... every good tree yields good fruit, but a rotten tree yields wicked fruit" (Matthew 7:16-17).*

This is true for all of us. Our fruit is a visual representation of our character, our very inner being, our core beliefs and everything we believe in. When we yield good fruit, we are a good tree; but when we yield wicked fruit, then we are a rotten tree. Our character, the character of man, is, in essence, rotten. We are born into sin, with a sinful nature, and we are taught to do good. We, by default, are rotten, and the Word confirms this for us (Romans 12:2-3). We are taught differently in this world because the world would have us believe that we are decent human beings and that we are by nature good people. If we believe this, then we are deceived, and the truth is not in us (see 1 John 3:18). The Word clearly says in that we are sinners (see Romans 3:23), so how does this make us good people?

Jeremiah 17:9 says:

> *"The heart is crooked above all, and desperately sick – who shall know it?"*

---

9 Merriam-Webster Dictionary, s.v. "character," https://www.merriam-webster.com/dictionary/character.

We, on the other hand, are taught and encouraged to follow our hearts. Do you see the problem here? We cannot do that because then we would be following a thing, our natural character, that is crooked above all things and desperately sick. I don't know about you, but I am surely not going to do that. I have followed my own inclincation too many times in my life and know that the end of this is always a disaster. It always leads to death and destruction.

"There is a way which seems right to man, but its end is the way of death" (Proverbs 14:12).

Consider the story of Job, who was a very successful person, the richest man in his area. The devil approached Yahweh and accused Him by saying that Job only served Him because of his wealth and success. Yahweh allowed the devil to "destroy" Job by inflicting punishment on him. His livestock was stolen, his crops were burned, and his children killed, yet Job did not speak ill of Yahweh. As the scripture puts it, he "did not sin with his lips" (Job 2:10). In the previous verse, when Job's wife approached him, she asked, "Do you still hold fast to your integrity?" You see, this was the mark of a man with character. He was allowed to be tested, even though he had done nothing wrong, and he remained steadfast and upright through it all. He "did not sin with his lips" during his ordeal and maintained his integrity. This is character, and this is what character does in times of adversity. It remains steadfast and faithful, even though it is not one's fault.

Consider this for a moment: we do things because they seem right to us, but the end of it is the way of death (see Proverbs 14:12). We want to listen to the world and do these things anyway. Are we stupid and ignorant? Or is this just our pride and arrogance getting in the way? I am going to say it is a combination of both. We lack the wisdom, so freely available, to be able to follow the way that leads to life and life in abundance.

Proverbs does not stop there, though; it continues and says this:

"Even in laughter the heart is in pain, and the end of that joy is heaviness" (Proverbs 14:13).

I understand why then people are filled with pain and a heaviness and why there is no healing. It is because they choose to follow their own hearts and the advice of men instead of being obedient to Elohim and the prompting of the Spirit of Elohim. We want to go to people who think they know the answers to life's problems and hear answers that seem good, but the end of their way is death. We need to go to the One who has put us together in our mother's womb and who intimately knows us and how we work (see Psalm 139).

Once again, we try the symptomatic relief approach because it is the easiest and the quickest way to get relief from the pain we are experiencing and the nightmare we are living in, but it does not solve the problem and does not deal with the issue. It is like when we notice a dark spot on an apple and try to cut it out, only to discover that the rest of the apple is rotten. That is us; we are rotten to the core. With training we become better at being decent human beings, but we are still sinners with sinful natures. It is written that "there is none righteous, no, not one" (Romans 3:10). This means that we have a sinful nature and through training and perseverance have been taught to distinguish between right and wrong. But we have to have been taught, and we have to exercise this training; otherwise, it is all in vain.

The Word of Elohim sums it up nicely:

"For I know that in me, that is in my flesh, dwells no good" (Romans 7:18).

This means that in and of ourselves there is no good. We need to understand and believe this because that is what is written. So, our earthly characters are bad and evil, sinful and deceitful, and we cannot trust in them to do any good. Remember, a bad tree can bear no good fruit (see Matthew 7:18). Fortunately, we have been redeemed by the blood of the Lamb, the ultimate sacrifice for you and me, so that we can live "perfect and straight" (see Job 1:1) before Him. So, if we are by nature sinful and have sinful characters, then how are we to overcome this character and how are we to develop it?

First, let's go to Romans 12:2, which states:

> *"And do not be conformed to this world, but be transformed by the renewing of your mind."*

Let us stop here for a moment. We are commanded to not conform any longer to this world, which means we are to do things differently to how the world does them. We have to think differently from the world because this is what the verse says. We are to renew our minds, and this renewing is done by the washing of the Word of Elohim (see Ephesians 5:26). The renewal here implies that our thoughts are to be influenced by either the Spirit of Elohim through the Word or by the devil through his lies. We are slaves to the things we are obedient to, says Romans 6:16. Thus, when we follow our sinful natures driven by the spirit of this world, then we are slaves to him. But when we follow the Spirit of Elohim who dwells in us and are obedient to Him, then we are slaves to the Spirit of Elohim.

So once again obedience is required on our part. This means we must be even more full of the Spirit of Elohim than we are of the spirit of this world, and we gain that Spirit when we allow the Word of Elohim to wash us and cleanse us.

> *"... Messiah also did love the assembly and gave Himself for it, in order to set it apart and cleanse it with the washing of water by the Word" (Ephesians 5:25-26).*

We are to change our thoughts and our thinking by being cleansed and by thinking like the Messiah did. The Word even says that we have the mind of Messiah (see 1 Corinthians 2:16). Therefore Romans 12:2 is quite clear: don't conform to this world, but "be transformed by the renewing of your mind." That happens when we allow the words of Elohim to be planted in our heart, or our spirit, and in our head. Then we will have the same mind as Yeshua, the very same thought processes. Romans 12:2 ends by saying that if we do not conform to this world and if we allow our minds to be transformed, then, and only then, will we be able to "prove what is that good and well-pleasing and perfect desire of Elohim." Why is our thought life so important and why does it need to be transformed? How does this have anything to do with character?

Simply put, our thoughts lead to actions, and actions are a visual display of our character. It is written in Proverbs that as a person reckons (thinks), so he or she is (see Proverbs 23:7). Our thoughts give birth to action. We are commanded in 2 Corinthians 10:5 to take every thought captive and make it obedient—not every action, but every thought—because when these thoughts take root in our minds, they lead to actions.

Our actions are a visual display of our character.

David is on his rooftop when he sees Bathsheba having a bath, and the Word says, "and the woman was very good to look at" (2 Samuel 11:2). I can only wonder what thoughts were going through David's head at this time, but there were definitely thoughts, for he decided to act on them by having this woman brought to him. The rest of the story is quite interesting to read.

Here is a great example of how our thoughts shape our actions. So, it is important to take control of our thought life and direct it in the right paths. When we have the mind of Yeshua, we are directed by the Spirit of Elohim into all truth (see 1 Corinthians 2:16; John 16:13).

Now that we have our thoughts under control, we need to develop the character of Yeshua as stated in Romans because by now we understand that our suffering leads to perseverance and our perseverance to character. But what is this character? Is it not being honest and kind and trustworthy? Partly so, but it is much more than that.

Galatians 5 gives us the best lesson on having our thoughts changed. The lesson starts by saying this:

> ***"Walk in the Spirit, and you shall not accomplish the lust of the flesh" (Galatians 5:16).***

When we submit ourselves to the authority of Elohim and the Spirit of Elohim and are led by the Spirit, then we turn away from doing worldly things. We repent, we have a change of mind, from the things we did before. But we have to walk in the Spirit. Galatians 5 continues to say that if we are led of the flesh, then we will do the things of the flesh. The list is quite sobering to read. Sadly, if we are led by the things of the flesh, when we are obedient to them, then we will not inherit the reign of Elohim.

If we are led of the Spirit, on the other hand, then we will display the character that Elohim requires of us and is spoken of in Romans 5. These fruits, the fruits of a good and righteous tree, are "love, joy, peace, patience, kindness, goodness, trustworthiness, gentleness, self-control" (Galatians 5:22-23). The more of the Spirit we have, the more obedient we are to the prompting of the Spirit. The more we allow the Spirit to permeate our souls, then the more of this fruit we will display. Remember, a tree has to be tended to, nurtured, watered and pruned in order for it to bear good fruit in season.

It is interesting to see that love again leads the pack, so to speak. Love is the most powerful motivator we have; it is the thing that drives us to do what needs to be done despite what the world says. It was the very thing that compelled Elohim to send His Son for us, so that we can be in right standing with Him. It was love that compelled Yeshua to die on the cross for us, primarily His love for His Father Elohim as well as His love for us. It will be the love we have for Elohim and His Son Yeshua and the love of the Spirit of Elohim that compels us to not conform any longer to this world but to be transformed by the renewing of our minds so that we can "prove what is that good and well-pleasing and perfect desire of Elohim" (Romans 12:2). We need to experience this life-changing love so that we can have the desire to live a life led of the Spirit and obedient to the commands of Yeshua, a

The Pain of Dealing

life that is pleasing to Elohim. This very love will drive us to grow and nurture the fruits of the Spirit mentioned in Galatians 5. This does not happen on its own accord; it is something that we have to work hard for so that the fruit of the Spirit can be evident in our lives.

How do we achieve this lofty goal, then? Is it even possible to attain these qualities? Yes, it is, and the process is a simple one, but one hard fought for. Remember that anything worthwhile stems from a hard-fought battle; cheap comes easy. The blueprint for our success is found here:

> **"His Mighty-like power has given us all we need for life and reverence [godliness], through the knowledge of Him who called us to esteem and uprightness" (2 Peter 1:3).**

We have been given *all* that we need for life. This means everything, not most, but everything. And when we fail in life, it is because we live in unbelief and because pride has taken root in our thinking. Also, it is because we failed to learn what the words of Elohim are. In other words, we failed to gain the knowledge of Elohim and of Yeshua. This passage of scripture carries on to say that we need to make sure that we "add to [our] belief uprightness, to uprightness knowledge, to knowledge self-control, to self-control endurance, to endurance reverence, to reverence brotherly affection, and to brotherly affection love" (2 Peter 1:5-7).

This scripture closes this section by saying that if these fruits are in us "and increase, they cause [us] to be neither inactive nor without fruit in the knowledge of our Master יהושע Messiah" (2 Peter 1:8).

Wow, doing these things will cause us not to be "inactive" or "without fruit." It is our responsibility to do these things and to add to them daily so that they grow and develop in us. We are responsible for this action, not the Spirit of Elohim or Yeshua or Elohim. *We* are commanded to do these things.

> *I remember once having a conversation with a new Christian who said that he did not have to do*

anything after he got saved because it was not up to him. So, my wife and I set about finding every command that we could in the New Testament. By the time we reached Acts, we had found hundreds of commands.

We need to understand this truth because we are commanded, and if we love Yeshua, then we will obey His commands. We need to be willing to be obedient and single-minded in our pursuit of this obedience because it is a life choice that will bring blessings to us. If, however, we choose to be disobedient, then we choose death and curses upon ourselves.

Hope

> *"'For I know the plans I am planning for you,' declares יהוה, 'plans of peace and not of evil, to give you a future and an expectancy'" (Jeremiah 29:11).*

I am sure we all have hope for something. Maybe it is a hope for a better job or a nicer car or maybe even for a fancier house. Maybe our hope is not for material things; maybe it is for a baby or a partner (which actually are material things, but you know what I mean). But what should we hope for? Or more importantly, who should our hope be in?

Let us briefly differentiate between belief (faith) and hope because they are, in reality, two very different things. We have already seen the scriptural meaning of belief (faith), so let us see what hope is. There are two very distinct differences between hope and faith.

Belief (faith) is in the present; hope is in the future. Belief (faith) is what we are doing right now, today, for today, while hope is what we foresee for the future. Belief is the expectancy of things that are hopefully going to happen in the future. For example, we believe that the Messiah will be coming back to earth—that is our belief today. This does not mean that it will necessarily happen today, but our hope is that it will happen in the future. We need to understand this so that we do not become despondent when what we hope for does not happen immediately. It is like planting an apple tree in the morning and expecting there to be fruit by the end of the day. That will not happen. But, if we tend to and nurture the tree and water it, then in due season we will reap the rewards of good fruit, or so we hope.

Belief is in the present; hope is in the future.

There is an expectation that when we do the right things, we will get our just reward. But what if something happens along the way? Say, for example, a storm comes along and the tree is damaged or destroyed, along with the expectation, due to no fault of our own? Things happen; life will throw you some curveballs along the way, so it is not a case of if, but when. We, however, have to deal with these things—hear what I say, we have to *deal* with it. Dealing is the hard part, it is the painful part, because we have to go back to the place of pain. But, in Yeshua, we have this hope that we can overcome these trials and tribulations. Our hope is not in man; it is in Elohim, His Son and His Set-Apart Spirit. We must exercise patience when expecting things to happen because, just like the apple tree bearing fruit in due season, we, too, will bear this fruit in due season.

The downside to this process—if there is a downside—is that the longer we wait and the longer the expectancy is, the higher the disappointment can be when our expectations are not met. "Hope deferred makes the heart sick," it says in Proverbs 13:12 of the New International Version, but this is because we hope in the "wrong things." I often hear people say that they are trusting Elohim for a new job or for a breakthrough of some sort, but I rarely hear anyone ever saying that they are trusting in Elohim ... period. The psalmist David says it best when he says, "we put our hope in You" (Psalm 33:22 NIV). This is the problem that we create for ourselves when we hope for things that might never happen, for then our hearts become sick.

This very thing happened to me a while back in my marriage when I expected something from my wife. While the expectation was realistic and within the boundaries of marriage, my wife was unable to meet my expectations and my heart became sick, to the point of wanting to leave the marriage. My problem was that, while expecting something from my wife, my hope was in her for that thing; thus, when this expectation was not met, it destroyed my confidence in her to the point of wanting to leave. I learned to have hope in Elohim, not for anything, but just in Him, and that change saved my marriage. I still have high expectations for my marriage and I still have to deal with disappointments, but my hope is in Elohim alone.

Belief (faith) is in the heart, in our spirit, and it is a given substance of what we expect, according to Hebrews 11. Belief (faith) is the substance, a real physical matter, of which something consists; it has a tangible, solid presence of what is expected; and it is the proof, something that induces certainty or establishes validity, of what is not yet seen.

We were on a mission trip in Mozambique when one of the Australian nationals lost her passport on a field trip. The village where we had been was not accessible by road; we had to fly in by helicopter to get there, which made going back rather difficult. In faith, I blurted out that the passport was not lost and that we would get it back for her —this was faith/belief—so I went and asked the pilot if he could stop by and collect the passport at the village on one of his next trips there. You see, I had said that that we would collect the passport at the village. I had not seen the passport; there was no way I could have contacted the villagers to ask them; but I was expectant that Elohim would produce the miracle. Anyway, the pilot returned from his trip, and I asked him for the passport. The passport was nowhere to be found. I was rather distraught, to say the least, and I had a little chat with Elohim about this. The Spirit of Elohim reminded me of what belief was and that it was the proof of what was not yet seen. I dried my teary eyes and, with renewed joy, went back to the Australian and told her that I would collect the passport on my next trip there. I went on the next available helicopter flight and arrived at the village. There was a big meeting going on, so we had to wait for the village chief to finish before we could ask anything, not to mention the language barrier that existed between me and the villagers. The meeting finished, and I was approached by a few men, whom I greeted, but before I could say anything, a young man, in English, said the following to me: "You must be here for the passport. I will send someone to fetch it for you." You have no idea of how much that boosted my faith and my confidence in Elohim. This was a clear case of what was expected and believing in it, though it was not yet seen.

Hope, on the other hand, is in the mind; it is part of the thought department. When we hope, we realize that the hope is not a given substance, it is not tangible, and it has no real physical matter. But our hope, the very thing we hope in, induces in us a certainty of what we believe in, and it establishes the validity of our belief. None of us have seen Elohim, yet we "believe that He is, and that He is a rewarder of those who earnestly seek Him" (Hebrews 11:6). It is this hope we have in Him that induces in us the certainty of, and validates, our belief. Hope is about waiting, and waiting means that the result is not instantaneous, that it may take time. Think about when we are having a baby. The process of procreation takes place, and we have faith that

EMOTIONAL WHOLENESS

the process will work. We are expectant of a miracle but have to wait for the miracle to happen and grow. We expect that the child will be born healthy even though we have not yet seen the evidence of it. I belabor the point a little here, but I want us to realize that hope is not instantaneous. It requires some time, and during this time, we are to remain expectant and display a good attitude while persevering to the end. Our hope should be in Elohim alone, not for anything, but just in Him. Remember, according to Joyce Meyer's *Battlefied of the Mind*, patience is not the ability to wait; it is the attitude we display while we are waiting. So, while we wait for the expectancy to become a reality, we had better display a good attitude, one filled with good fruit because of the Spirit of Elohim in us.

Hope is in our heads; it is part of the thoughts that we have. Hope remembers that as we think, so we are (see Proverbs 23:7). We believe in our heart, our spirit, but we hope in our head. Why is that important? If hope is in our head, then it can influence our thoughts that are formed and developed there, control our emotions through those thought processes, and drive our decisions based on that reasoning and deduction (mostly). Sometimes we allow our emotions to drive us, but that is because we have not yet established the art of keeping our emotions in check. We allow our emotions to run rampant and make emotional decisions, most of which we regret. We need to get to the point where our thoughts and emotions are driven by the Spirit of Elohim in us. In other words, when we are dealing with negative emotions—and we will—we must allow the Spirit of Elohim to flow in us and the fruits of the Spirit to be evident in us. So, when we are not doing well, we still, according to James 1:2, "count it all joy," a fruit of the Spirit. But when there is no joy, then it is impossible to do so. This is a principle of life: you cannot give what you do not have.

So why don't we have hope? It is because we have allowed our emotions and thoughts to take control of our lives. We live under the control of our fleshly selves instead of under the control of the Spirit of Elohim. Remember, it is written:

> ***"For Elohim has not given us a spirit of cowardice, but of power and love and of self-control" (2 Timothy 1:7).***

We have just to exercise it. Exercise requires effort, and there will be pain in this effort.

Think about when you exercise for the first time in a while. When you are done, it may hurt, but give it a day or two, and then it really hurts. However, as you progress, the pain subsides, and you push through because you have a goal that you want to achieve. You expect the result of your hard work will be a healthier, better-looking body, and you hope that the results will be realized even though you have not yet seen them.

The same is true for our emotional and spiritual well-being. We should be just as enthusiastic and motivated to achieve spiritual and emotional growth, even though there will be pain, because we are expectant of and hope for the healing that we so desire.

Hope looks to the future; it is not for the present or for the past. It is for what lies ahead. Philippians 4:13 says that we are to forget "what is behind" and reach "out for what lies ahead." This directive implies a hope for the future, a hope in things that we have not yet seen or experienced, a hope that we are more than conquerors and that we can do all things through Yeshua who strengthens us (see Hebrews 11:1; Romans 8:37; Philippians 4:13). It is a hope that we have been given everything that we need for life and for uprightness through the Spirit of Elohim (see 2 Peter 1:3). Without hope we are doomed; without hope we are unable to believe in the very One who created us and who sent His Son for us, the One who loved us so much that He sacrificed His Son for our sins. We need this hope in order to believe. The basis of this hope is in Romans 8:28, where it is written:

> **"And we know that all matters work together for good to those who love Elohim, to those who are called according to his purpose."**

If we love Elohim with all our heart, all our being and all our mind (see Matthew 22:37), then these matters will happen. Our hope will come to fruition and our expectations will be met. The criteria for hope, as with anything else written in the scriptures, is love. In 1 Corinthians 13, Paul speaks about the qualities of love. He defines love for us and ends the chapter by saying that "belief, expectation, and love remain – these three. But the greatest of these is love" (verse 13). In the next chapter, Paul starts by saying that we need to "pursue love, and earnestly seek the spiritual gifts" (1 Corinthians 14:1). So, for us, hope is grounded in love, the very unfailing love that Elohim has for us. Everything we do, we should do because we love Elohim and are called according to His purpose (see Romans 8:28).

Hope is in the head, while belief is in the heart, meaning that our faith is in our spirit being because it is by faith, by belief, that we are saved through the grace of Elohim (see Ephesians 2:8). Hope is in the head, in our thoughts and that part of our brain that deals with logical reasoning and emotions. Because hope is in the head, it is subject to attack, unrelenting attacks, by the father of all lies. Hope is the desire we have, with expectation, of obtainment and fulfilment.

Hope is in the head, while belief is in the heart.

Because we believe in our heart, the heart is protected by the Spirit of Elohim. It is for this very reason that we are commanded to renew our minds, not our hearts. We then need to protect our heads, or minds, from the attacks of the father of all lies. We do so by putting on the helmet of salvation, which is part of the armor of Elohim that we discussed earlier. Another resource I recommend, which explains this battlefield excellently, is Joyce Meyer's *Battlefield of the Mind*.[10] The real attack happens here because it is the easiest place to be attacked.

In a military context, an attack always takes place at the weakest point. The enemy, who will have done his reconnaissance, will find the weakest point to attack, then attack. No good soldier attacks the enemy at their strongest point, but always at the weakest point.

Take a look at what happened in the garden of Eden to Eve as described in Genesis 3. The devil did not attack Eve at her strong point,

---

10 Joyce Meyer, *Battlefield of the Mind*. Warner Books, 1995

The Pain of Dealing

but at her weak point. He planted the seed of doubt in her head, not in her heart. You see, the devil knows where our weak point is, but so does Elohim, and it is for this reason that He commands us to be renewed by the washing of the Word (see Ephesians 5:26). The very basis of the word *repent* is to change the way we think about something, so we need to take note that the battlefield is in the mind, not in our spirit.

By putting on the full armor of Elohim, we can go into battle and withstand the onslaught of the evil one. When we have on the helmet of deliverance, then our minds are protected. But it is not enough to have this helmet; we are commanded to put on the full armor of Elohim. If we have to go into battle—and we do—then let us be prepared to do so. We need to have all the equipment that has been provided by Elohim for us to be successful in battle. But we fail to appropriate and exercise this equipment.

No one in their right mind will equip their children without the proper training and use of that equipment. Much like learning to drive a car, you will not allow your children to drive without a valid permit and without the necessary training. It would be like sending them to an early grave if you did that. Similarly, if we do not use and train with the full armor of Elohim, then we are going to our deaths. We have been given these weapons so that we can stand against the schemes of the devil, Ephesians 6:11 says. This passage in Ephesians continues on to say that we need to be "praying at all times, with all prayer and supplication in the Spirit, watching in all *perseverance* and supplication for all the set-apart ones" (6:18). So, having gone through all of the earlier discussion, let us understand the context of perseverance in our pursuit of wholeness. All of this is a process that we need to follow to achieve the end result. We must have this vision of what we need to be in Elohim, according to His Word. We must have a clear understanding of His vision for us by the renewing of our minds and the washing of the Word of Elohim, as Ephesians 5:26 says. This process, like any other, if followed, will produce the desired result in its time.

Psalm 1 tells us that we are blessed if we do not "walk in the counsel of the wrong, and shall not stand in the path of sinners," and that we will be like the "tree planted by the rivers of water, that yields its fruit in its season" (Psalm 1:1, 3).

Again, this is a process. It is not going to happen automatically; there is no magic wand to be waved so that we can be healed and set free in an instant. There is a process, fueled by love—our love for Elohim, His Son Yeshua and His Spirit—that compels us to be obedient to His Word and to obey His commands. This process requires us to believe in Elohim, not for anything, but just in Him; it means that we believe that He is and that He is a rewarder of those who diligently seek Him (see Hebrews 11:6). In order for us to believe, we need to make a decision that the Elohim we serve is mighty and powerful; we need to decide that He sent His Son, Yeshua, to die for us on the cross so that we may have life and have it in abundance. Making such a stand does not mean that our lives will be perfect, but it does mean that, through Yeshua Messiah and the Spirit of Elohim, we have been empowered for life and for reverence through Him. We have to believe, and our belief has to be fueled by love, the very love we have received from on high.

In 1 John 5 it is written that we know what love for Elohim is:

"For this is the love for Elohim, that we guard His commands, and His commands are not heavy, because everyone having been born of Elohim overcomes the world. And this is the overcoming that has overcome the world: our belief" (1 John 5:3-4).

I leave you with this scripture, where Yeshua tells His disciples:

"These words I have spoken to you, that in Me you might have peace. In the world you have pressure, but take courage, I have overcome the world" (John 16:33).

Chapter Eight
The Path of Healing

Heal

"A rejoicing heart causes good healing, but a stricken spirit dries the bones" (Proverbs 17:22).

Healing is a process, and like any process, it requires a few elements. The definition of process shows us that it is "a series of actions or steps taken in order to achieve a particular end."[1] So it is with healing: we need to take certain actions or steps in order to achieve it. What are these steps, and what do they look like? We already know what the problem is; it has been revealed to us through much prayer, intercession and meditation. We are aware that the problem exists, and now we have to do something to fix the problem.

For example, suppose you go out for a run or a walk, the conditions are wet and slippery, and you fall. While lying there on the ground, you realize something is wrong with your arm or leg. You inspect the injured part of your body and see that it is lying at a very odd angle, which, of course, is not normal. There is a revelation that something is wrong.

---

[1] Microsoft Bing, s.v. "process" accessed June 15, 2021, https://www.bing.com/.

You dial 911 and the paramedics arrive. They get you stabilized and into the ambulance for your trip to the ER. Once you are at the hospital, an x-ray is taken of the damaged part and establishes that there is indeed a broken bone. Bear in mind that there are different types of breaks that require different treatment in order to heal; there is no "one approach fixes all" here. So, the diagnosis is made, then the doctor has to manipulate the broken bone back into its original place. This step will hurt quite badly, but it must be done. The setting of the bone is done and there is pain, but after a few hours the pain subsides and the healing process begins to take place in your body. Six weeks later the bone will have been restored and be even stronger in the restored area than in any other part of the bone.

Take this scenario and understand what would have happened if you had not gone to the ER and had the arm seen to. It would have started healing improperly. It would have mended askew and instead of being pain-free, you would have suffered with it for the rest of your life. You would have had constant pain and suffering, and the quality of your life would be miserable, to say the least. Our normal lives are like this; we get damaged emotionally, we get beat up, and instead of going to the "ER" to see the Physician who can heal us, we try and do all sorts of other things in the hope of getting better.

> *I am reminded of a popular story about Henry Ford. His factory was built, and the electrical genius of the day had ensured that the electricity was put in and working properly. One day, however, the electricity failed, and Ford called in some other electrician to fix the problem. This man was not successful. In desperation, Ford called on Steinmetz, the electrical genius, and asked if he could solve the problem. Steinmetz came in and tinkered for a few hours, and when he flicked the switch, it worked. Ford received a bill from Steinmetz for the astronomical amount of ten thousand dollars. Ford sent the invoice back to Steinmetz with a little note attached, saying, "Don't you think that is rather expensive for just tinkering*

around?" Steinmetz sent the invoice back with his own note, saying, "For tinkering around, ten dollars. For knowing where to tinker, nine thousand nine hundred and ninety dollars." ... Henry Ford paid the bill.[2]

There is a very clear indication of how things should get done here. When we become damaged, we need to seek the help of those who can fix the problem. It is of no use to go to an optometrist when we have kidney problems. We need to find the specialists who can solve the problem and help us to heal. So, in the case of our emotional damage, we tend to find people who can help us—or who we think can help us—instead of going to the One who can help us: the very One who put us together, who knit us together in our mother's womb; the very Physician who made sure that that the million nerve endings growing from our brain met up with the million nerve endings growing from our eyes so that we would have sight. The very One who gave us so much human DNA that if we were to tie them together and stretch them out, the strands would go to the moon and back about 109,000 times.[3] Instead, we go to therapists to talk about our problems and try and delve into an area so complex that humans do not understand it, wanting to believe what they tell us. I would rather go to the very Creator of this whole system, who put us together and knit us in our mother's womb, the very One who created us from dust and breathed life into us. He is my Physician.

Now, I am not discounting modern medicine in any way. I am saying that there are areas of our lives that humans cannot heal. It is only the great Physician Himself who can do that.

Take, for example, the case of a well-known prophet, Graham Cooke, who was scheduled to speak at a meeting. He told that while waiting for the event to start, Elohim told him to go over to a young lady

---

2 Today in the Word, MBI, April, 1990, pg. 27, as quoted in "Knowing Where to Tinker," Bible.org, accessed June 15, 2021, https://bible.org/illustration/knowing-where-tinker.
3 "How long would your entire DNA stretch out?" *Answers.com*, December 13, 2010.

> *sitting in one of the seats and tell her that He, Elohim, did not like mommies and daddies either. This was a strange thing, and Cooke argued with Elohim that it was not a good idea. Elohim insisted, and Cooke went over to this lady and told her exactly what Elohim had told him to say. The woman broke down in tears and, through Elohim's counsel, it was revealed that she had been sexually abused by a family member who played the game of "mommies and daddies."*[4]

This highlights the point that the very One who put us together can restore us to wholeness and knows where to tinker. The best thing is, He won't even bill us for the work. As a matter of fact, He paid the bill for us in advance.

Belief

The first and most important element is belief. The story of Yeshua's death and resurrection is to stir up and test your faith; it is to awaken within your spirit the greatest gift given to us. We have long forgotten the magnitude of this selfless act; nevertheless, we must understand that belief is the key element in the restoration process. Why, do you ask? Without belief, it is impossible to please Elohim. It is written:

> ***"But without belief it is impossible to please Him, for he who comes to Elohim has to believe that He is, and that He is a rewarder of those who earnestly seek Him" (Hebrews 11:6).***

Hebrews 11:1 clearly defines faith or belief for us. It says:

> ***"And belief is the substance of what is expected, the proof of what is not seen."***

---

[4] David Ravenhill, "Tell her 'God hates mommies and daddies' (what?!)," an excerpt about Graham Cooke from Ravenhill's book *Surviving the Anointing*, last modified June 5, 2014, witness.org/index.php/categories/sound-of-gods-voice/item/67-tell-her-god-hates-mommies-and-daddies-what.

So, we believe in Elohim because Elohim Himself has given to each of us a measure of belief. We have not yet seen Him; we have not yet seen the Messiah or the Spirit of Elohim, yet we believe, or say we believe, in Them. This is not because of us, but because of Elohim, who has given us a measure of belief (see Romans 12:3). Hebrews 11 continues to cite story after story of the consequences of belief; Noah is a great example. Genesis chapters 6 through 8 tell the story. Noah was told to build an ark because it was going to rain, and rain was not a known concept because the earth was watered from the ground. Imagine the ridicule he must have endured when he told people why he was building a boat. It took him approximately a hundred years to finish. You can imagine how the people mocked him and how his belief was tested.

Day after day he labored on in belief of Elohim, in the substance of what was expected, and in the proof of what was not seen. His obedience is also a great example of suffering as mentioned in Romans 5. Noah suffered daily from the ridicule, but he persevered and built character in this process (see Romans 5:3 NIV). Noah clung to his faith as if his life depended on it, which it did, and not only his life but also the lives of the others who went with him.

The second element of this belief or faith is obedience. So what if Noah believed in Elohim? So what if Noah knew that Elohim was the Almighty? He still could have done nothing with the instructions given to him by Elohim. Then you and I would not be here today because all of humankind would have been destroyed by the flood. James 2:20 states that belief without "works is dead." If Noah believed but did not act on that belief, it would be dead. Obedience is a key ingredient in belief; we need to act on the belief, and the key driver to obedience is love. Our motivation to want to be obedient to Yeshua is driven by love. It is written:

> **"This is the love, that we walk according to His commands ..." (2 John 1:6).**

If we love Him, then we will obey His commands. You see, love is the most powerful motivator on this earth. Without love, the Messiah would not have given His life for us. Without love, Elohim would not have sent His Son to die for us. We need to grasp the power and the enormity of love because it is impossible to understand these things without it. Obedience is not a result of having a slave mentality, as many people would like us to believe. Rather, obedience is a result of love, the love of Elohim given to us so that we may have life in abundance. We need to be obedient to the calls and commands of the Spirit of Elohim as He works in us and through us so that we can be made whole and complete and lacking in nothing (see James 1:4).

Love is the most powerful motivator on this earth.

We also can read in Matthew 8 the story of the Roman captain who came to Yeshua and spoke to Him about his servant who was ill. Here is a prime example of faith in action. This captain believed that Yeshua could heal his servant, even though he did not believe in a Jewish Messiah; he knew that Yeshua had the authority to affect the healing. Yeshua, after performing the miracle, marvelled at the captain. He turned to the crowd following Him and said, "Truly, I say to you, not even in Yisra'el have I found such great belief!" (Matthew 8:10) Wow, what a slap in the face for the followers of Yeshua, the believers and disciples. Here is an unbeliever who believes greater than those of the covenant. You see, belief is the major hurdle we must surmount to receive our healing and our wholeness. We need to become like the captain and expect the healing to happen, even though we have not yet seen it. Faith moves Elohim to act, and "without belief it is impossible to please Him" (Hebrews 11:6).

The second element worth mentioning in the story of the captain is that during the initial exchange when Yeshua says that He will go to the man's house, the captain stops Him, saying that he is not worthy for Yeshua to be under his roof. He realizes that he is dealing with greatness, with a man of Elohim; he continues on and says that he, too, is a man of authority. So, he recognizes that Yeshua has authority as well. But he not only recognizes, he also knows, for as a man of authority, he knows full well what authority looks like, what it acts like and what it does. His knowledge of authority coupled with his belief led to the healing of his servant. You and I would do well to know this authority and to believe it, too, for without this belief, we know that it is impossible to please Elohim (see Hebrews 11:6).

How do we get to the place of knowing this authority and of using it to please Elohim and do His desire? We need to understand what authority is and to whom it belongs before we can answer this question. Back in Genesis when Elohim created the world and everything in it, He decided that man was going to be the ruler of this earthly kingdom. The man Elohim created was given the authority to rule over the creation. So, although all authority belongs to Elohim, He has given us the authority to do things on His behalf. We know the rest of the story: man sinned and the fall happened, and with that fall our authority was damaged, but not taken away. That means we still have authority on this earth because we still rule it, but because of sin we have destroyed the very thing we were given authority over. Take, for example, birth. Elohim gave us authority to procreate on His behalf, to create human life for His glory, but we, as people, have destroyed this charge. We have legalized abortions, the "legitimate" killing of a baby, because we saw fit to do so. We use sex, which is a powerful authority, for all sorts of degenerate and vile things. We have taken the authority given to us by Elohim and abused it for our own perverted entertainment.

So, what is this authority and where does it come from? The word *authority* in Greek is *exousia*. It comes from the Greek verb *exesti,* meaning "it is lawful" or right.[5] Therefore, authority is the power to command what is right or lawful. Spiritual authority comes from above, through the Spirit of Elohim. Yeshua said, "All authority has been given to Me in heaven and on earth" (Matthew 28:18). Authority is not something we take; it is something we are given. In Matthew 9 the story is told of Yeshua healing a lame man. Yeshua is stopped by the belief of the people who are with the lame man, and He says to him, "Take courage, son, your sins have been forgiven" (verse 2). This is extremely interesting and important to note. Yeshua did not tell the

---

5 *The KJV New Testament Greek Lexicon*, s.v. "exesti," accessed June 24, 2021, https://www.biblestudytools.com/lexicons/greek/kjv/exesti.html.

man that he was healed; He told him that his sins had been forgiven. In verse 6 Yeshua says, "But in order for you to know that the Son of Adam possesses authority on earth to forgive sins," He then tells the lame man, "Rise, take up your bed, and go to your house." Two things happened here.

The first thing is that Yeshua is stopped by the belief of the people. In other words, our belief is what causes things to happen. Secondly, Yeshua forgives the man his sins. He, then, in authority, tells the man to get up and go home. This confirms to us that we need belief to be healed and that we need to be forgiven of our sins. There are more accounts of Yeshua exercising this authority, the power to do what is right or lawful, in the Word.

In another story, the man with the unclean spirit living in him sees Yeshua from afar and bows down to Him, not knowing who He is, but the unclean spirit living in him knows and recognizes the authority that Yeshua had been given. (Read Mark 5.) You see that authority is not something we take; it is something we are given to exercise. I have heard people praying that they take authority over something when they should have been exercising this authority. Authority is to be applied over every situation in our lives; we exercise the authority given to us from above over all spiritual matters and believe that this authority has the power to do what the Word of Elohim says it will do. Just like the Roman captain, we are to know, understand and use authority to do the desire of Elohim in our lives.

If we knew what to do with the authority given to us, we would not be dealing with the majority of problems we do. We would be able to deal with everything that is thrown at us and be successful. Why do we then fail, if we have been given all authority to be victorious? The answer lies in the fact that we do not understand authority and so do not live it.

Understanding authority is the easiest part of this problem. We are told in the Word of Elohim that we have been given everything that we need for life and for uprightness by His divine power, the Spirit of Elohim (see 2 Peter 1:3). We are told that "we are more than overcomers through Him" (Romans 8:37) and that we "have strength to do all, through Messiah who empowers" us (Philippians 4:13). The key phrase here is *through Him*—that means through nothing of our own but through His power and His authority. Everything that has authority in the spiritual realm is through Yeshua Messiah and through the power of the Spirit of Elohim, given by Elohim. We fail at exercising authority because we try and do it in our own power, and we should know that this is doomed to failure every time.

> *I have seen this truth many times in my own life. When I have faced trials and temptations and submitted myself to Elohim, then I was able to withstand and endure the trial and temptation. When I faced them on my own strength, however, then I failed miserably. I remember once while I was playing golf on my own, I had an attack in my mind from the devil. It came out of nowhere, as I was not thinking about the matter I was being attacked on. I instantly realized that this was an attack. While walking down the fairway, I mimicked putting on the armor of Elohim in preparation for battle. It must have been quite a sight for others who might have seen this spectacle. Here I was, walking down the course on my own, putting on imaginary armor, and wielding my shield and sword. As funny as it might have looked, it worked because the attack did not last long, and the devil remained defeated. There also have been many times that I failed to submit to the authority of Elohim and to exercise it according to His commands, and each time I failed dismally.*

The Word of Elohim is very clear when it says in James 4:7, "So then subject yourselves to Elohim. Resist the devil and he shall flee from you." We are commanded to subject ourselves to Elohim—that means daily. Every hour and every minute of every day, we are to be subject to the authority and power of Elohim. We are commanded to resist the devil; we are to take an active role in this battle and resist the father of all lies. The very definition of resist is to "withstand the action or effect of" something,[6] or in this case, someone. When we resist, we are exercising the authority that has been given to us through the Spirit of Elohim by Elohim to combat the schemes of the devil. You have to love the verse in Ephesians 6 before the ones that tell us about the armor of Elohim, where it says, "For the rest, my brothers, be strong in the Master and in the mightiness of His strength" (verse 10).

We fail because we try to do things in our strength, in our understanding and in our own might and power. We will never succeed; we lack the authority and power to do so because we are disobedient to the Word of Elohim. Proverbs 3:5 is quite clear when it says that we are to "trust in יהוה with all your heart, and lean not on your own understanding." We are to trust in Yahweh with all our heart—all our spirit-being is to trust *in* Yahweh, not for anything, just in Him—and we are not to lean on, or depend on, our own understanding, especially of things of a spiritual nature.

> ***"Because we do not wrestle against flesh and blood, but against principalities, against authorities, against the world-rulers of the darkness of this age, against spiritual matters of wickedness in the heavenlies" (Ephesians 6:12).***

This is quite a statement. Our battle is not against flesh and blood, although we certainly feel it there and try and fight it there. Why? Because the world tells us that it is so. Scientists and doctors tell us that there is medication for depression or medication for multiple personality disorders and medication for every type of disorder that has been discovered. We want to believe it because we think that that medication is a quick fix to our problems, that it will take away the pain. Now, this may be accurate to a degree; the pain might subside, but the cause is never taken care of. We like the symptomatic relief without the actual solving of the problem because, in solving the problem, in dealing with the actual issue, we need to do something for ourselves

---

[6] Microsoft Bing, s.v. "resist," accessed June 16, 2021, https://www.bing.com/.

and take responsibility for our own lives. That is hard, but not impossible, for although something may be impossible to man, "with Elohim all is possible" (Matthew 19:26). When we believe what the words of Elohim have to say and are obedient to them, meaning we actually do what they say, then we will reap the fruits of what we have sown.

> *There was a man who had been diagnosed with dissociative identity disorder, or in older terms, multiple personality disorder. The church that he was attending offered counseling for this disorder, and when I read the training manual I was horrified at its content. The people afflicted with this disorder were told that it was a gift from Elohim so that they could cope with life and that if they stayed in therapy for the rest of their lives, then they would be okay. Now, I am sure that this is a lie from the very pit of hell because how would Yahweh, who loved us so much that He gave His only Son to die for us to set us free, gift us with this disorder? I cannot for one moment believe that Elohim uses a disorder to create healing. It is clearly written that "Elohim is not Elohim of disorder but of peace" (1 Corinthians 14:33). Therefore, the opposite of peace is disorder and the opposite of disorder is peace. How can anyone think that Elohim can use a disorder to give us peace and to heal us? Has the church gone mad? And then to spend the rest of your life in therapy is foolish talk because it is written that if "the Son makes you free, you shall be free indeed" (John 8:36). This does not mean that you need therapy for the rest of your life; it means you need to repent and be born again.*

The preceding verses to John 8:36 are very important as they lead up to this point. Yeshua is talking to the Jews and says to them, "If you stay in My Word, you are truly My taught ones, and you shall know the truth, and the truth shall make you free" (John 8:31-32).

I want to throw in an important note here regarding the use of the word *shall*. In legal terms, *shall* is an imperative command. It is not merely a suggestion or a hint to do something. So once again the command has been given, as in "you *shall* know the truth, and the truth *shall* make you free."

Shall is not a suggestion.

So, going back to the passage in John, one of the reasons we fail to receive healing is that we fail to follow the process set out for us. Firstly, we must stay in His Word, which implies that everything we do, we do according to the words of Elohim, diligently following them and obeying them, because belief without works is in itself dead (see James 2:20). Believing in the words of Elohim is the first step in this process because if we stay in His Word, then we are truly His "taught ones," meaning we are truly His disciples, and disciples are followers. So, if we are in His Word, then we are His followers, followers of Yeshua. And if we are followers of Yeshua, then, and only then, we will know the truth, and it *shall* make us free. The reason we are not free from a lot of our disorder in life is that we are not truly followers of Yeshua and do not know the truth. The words of Elohim are the truth, the only truth, and are therefore the only authority we have for the tearing down of strongholds in our lives. (See John 17:17; 2 Corinthians 10:5.) The bondages we have, the afflictions we suffer and the disorders that have invaded us can and shall be broken down.

This biblical authority we have can only be in operation if we fulfill every criterion for it to be met. We cannot expect this authority to operate when we don't follow the conditions that are set. There are certain things that Yahweh has declared for all of us, whether we are born again or not, but the conditions for them to be in operation still have to be met. The Roman captain, who was not a follower of Yeshua, knew and understood the authority that was in Him; he met all of the criterion for this authority to be in operation, and the end result spoke for itself. The basis of this authority was belief. He believed that Yeshua was, and still is, the Son of Elohim, and that alone was the requirement for the spiritual authority to take place over death. How much more does Elohim care for His own children then? It is written:

> *"Are not two sparrows sold for a copper coin? And not one of them falls to the ground without your Father. And even the hairs of your head are all numbered. So do not fear, you are worth more than many sparrows"* (Matthew 10:29-31).

This passage says, simply, that we are far more valuable than the sparrows of the air and that the Father cares for us more than that, to the point where He wants to see us healed and set free, so that we shall be free indeed. We have the authority in us, through the Messiah Yeshua, to do all that we are commanded to do, but it has to be through Him and not through ourselves or others. Understanding this authority is a vital step in the healing process; we need to believe in Him in the process in order for healing to take place.

> *I want to share a story here of belief with works that I heard about. Heidi Baker had established a mission station in Mozambique and had several ministries going on at one time, one of which was caring for orphaned babies and toddlers. Volunteers would show up from around the globe to help out with the mission, and amazing work was being done. There was one baby who was desperately ill, and one of the nurses said that she needed a hot water bottle in order for the baby to survive. However, Mozambique is a tropical country, so there was no need for hot water bottles. Thus it was not impossible to get, but highly improbable. A container had arrived earlier that day with gifts and foods from donors, and as they were unpacking this container,*

> *there was one gift that had been sent from England with a note attached saying that although she knew this was a most unlikely gift, Elohim had told her to send one, so she did: a hot water bottle. Of course, the baby survived. The story is in itself remarkable, but think of the woman who sent it. She likely had bought this gift some weeks prior at the prompting of the Spirit of Elohim and had sent it just at the right time for it arrive on that day in order to save the life of the baby. This thrills me and boosts my belief because it is a real example of belief, of obedience and works in action. Imagine what it did to the nurse in Mozambique and imagine what it did to the woman in England, if she ever knew what had happened.*

Belief and Commitment
Secondly, and this is a big one, is that we fail at following through not only because we fail to remember the principle of the path and are not committed, but also because we do not truly believe in what we are trying to achieve, which leads to a lack of deep conviction.

If we really believed that being healthy is advantageous to us and those around us, then we would be able to commit to following a healthy lifestyle because of a deep conviction in this belief. If we really believed that being excellent will benefit us and those around us, then we would be committed to excelling … I am truly hoping that the lightbulb is going on here.

I think we are often simply infatuated with the ideas that we see in magazines or on billboards. I mean, who would not want a nice beach body or great abs or that nice car, etc.? But infatuation will not help us reach those goals; only truly believing in our abilities to actually reach them will help us. Infatuation is not a firm belief; it is the romantic notion that we really like what we see … until we have to stop eating the junk foods and exercise or study instead of going to the all-night party. Having a firm belief is the best start, and coupling that firm belief to a deep conviction will help us get from where we are to where we want to go.

When you believe, believe it with all your being because, if you don't, you will not achieve what you intend to achieve and instead will be "like a wave of the sea driven and tossed by the wind" without direction (James 1:6).

Forgiveness

> *"Let all bitterness, and wrath, and displeasure, and uproar, and slander be put away from you, along with all evil. And be kind towards one another, tenderhearted, forgiving one another, as Elohim also forgave you in Messiah" (Ephesians 4:31-32).*

We are commanded to put away all bitterness, rage and anger. Not try our best to deal with it or go and see a counsellor and talk about it; we are to get rid of it. Just a quick side note here: Have you noticed that nowhere in the scriptures does it ever ask us to do something? We are always commanded to do it. Go have a look for yourself. We are told by Yeshua in John 14:23 that if we love Him, we will guard His commands. So, when we are told to get rid of all bitterness, anger and rage, it is best we do so because it will demonstrate our love for Yeshua. The scriptures say that we love Him because He first loved us (see 1 John 4:19) ... and He loved us so much that He willingly died on the cross for us so that our sins could be forgiven. If this was the model set by Yeshua, then we should follow the example and do the same thing.

We often are not healed because we have unforgiveness in our hearts towards other people.

> *I remember a case in Toronto that I witnessed about a man who had been involved in a vehicle collision with another motorist and had been badly injured in the crash. The other motorist was to blame, and this man underwent a few surgeries, but his injury would not heal properly. He had had prayer for the injury many times but did not receive healing.*

> *At this particular evening meeting, the pastor, who was praying for him, asked him some questions about the incident and determined whose fault it was. He did so at the leading of the Set-Apart Spirit. When it was determined that the other motorist was at fault, the pastor asked him if he was angry at the other driver. The man answered yes, and the pastor told the man that he needed to repent of his unforgiveness and forgive the other driver. The man did so, and he was instantly healed.*

Unforgiveness is a sin that can hinder our progress and our walk. When we fail to forgive, we choose death and suffer the consequences of our actions.

> *I had a similar experience when I was saved. I was being counseled by a friend, and one day when I arrived at his house, he gave me a chocolate bar that had a message on the wrapper. The message simply read, "Forgive me." I thought it was rather strange and asked him why I needed to forgive him. He looked at me and said that the message was for me, that I needed to forgive me. It was a watershed moment, literally and figuratively, as I realized that even though I was forgiven by Yeshua, I had failed to forgive myself for all the colorful things I had done in my life. This unforgiveness was a hindrance to my healing, to my being set free and to my wholeness.*

When we fail to forgive, even ourselves, then we fail to receive forgiveness. It is clearly written that if we do not forgive others, including ourselves, then Elohim will not forgive us (see Matthew 6:15).

Acts 3:19 says, "Repent therefore and turn back, for the blotting out of your sins, in order that times of refreshing might come from the presence of the Master." The New International Version of this

The Path of Healing

verse says to "repent, then, and turn to God, so that your sins may be wiped out, that times of refreshing may come from the Lord." The first step in this process is to repent. We have covered this before, but let us refresh our memories here. Repent means to change the way we think about something. So we need to change the way we think about our behavior, about what we say, about what we do, about what we think. It all starts with a thought process. Forgiveness is the result of a thought process because once the transgression has been revealed by the Set-Apart Spirit, then we need to do something about it. We need to act on that thought. We need to make a choice. We might think that we cannot forgive because what was done to us was so harmful that we could never do it. Then we are calling the Messiah a liar and His Word is untrue. It is as simple as that.

It is written that we can do *all*—not some, or only the things we are good at, or just the things we want to do—but "*all*, through Messiah who empowers" us (Philippians 4:13). It is the Messiah who has given us the strength. You and I may not have the strength on our own to do it, but when we anchor ourselves in the written Word and the risen Messiah, then we have the power, the same power that raised up the Messiah from the dead, to do *all* through Him who empowers us. The second thing to note is that we can these things through Yeshua, not with Him but through Him. This truth is important because when we try and do things in our own strength, then we will possibly fail because we do not have the strength. This is where belief is vital. If we believe, then we can receive, but without the belief that the written Word is true, we cannot receive, and if we cannot receive, then we cannot give.

Belief, if it does not have works, is in itself dead (see James 2:20). In other words, we need to produce evidence of our belief. If we fail to do so, then we are liars and the truth is not in us (see 1 John 2:4). We then, by our actions, nullify His death on the cross and the work that was done for us by the Messiah. We need to believe; we need belief to put into action our works. Without belief, forgiveness is not possible. Yeshua says it clearly: "If you are able to believe, all is possible to him who believes" (Mark 9:23). Once again, if we are able to believe, then *all* things are possible to those who do. Forgiveness will only happen

EMOTIONAL WHOLENESS

when we believe the written Word.

Thus, we need to repent firstly of our own sin and secondly—I would suggest—of our unbelief, for we desperately need to do so. We then need to believe that we can do *all* things because of our belief. Once we have received forgiveness, we can then give it to others because now we have it to give. We have received; now we can give.

Once we have received forgiveness, we can give it to others.

What happens when we don't forgive? The answer is simple: then we are not forgiven. We will not be forgiven in the same way we fail to forgive. It is clearly written, "Forgive us our debts, as we forgive our debtors" (Matthew 6:12). Furthermore, the Word says that "if you forgive men their trespasses, your heavenly Father shall also forgive you. But if you do not forgive men their trespasses, neither shall your Father forgive your trespasses" (Matthew 6:14-15). It is very clear that we will not receive any forgiveness of our trespasses if we fail to forgive others who have trespassed against us. This is a severe consequence of our choices. And we do have a choice in this matter. "I have set before you life and death, the blessing and the curse," it is written in Deuteronomy 30:19—the blessing when we obey the commands of Elohim and the curse if we do not obey the commands of Elohim. It is very simple. We obey and we get blessed or we disobey and we get cursed.

Life and Death Choices

I was watching a television series when, as usual, something was said that triggered a train of thought and a stirring in my heart to pen those thoughts on paper. This is what I do enjoy about life and the experiences we have, even the negative ones, because we can learn and grow from each one.

I wrote, "Death … and the Life we Live."

I in no way intend to be depressing and dreary or sad and morbid. This book is intended to be a motivational catalyst to get you to re-think life, or at least some aspects thereof.

We are all born ... a given fact, and it is an important day for all of us. The second most important day is when we find out why. You have read about that before in a previous discusson. In this moment on earth, though, in this thing we call life, there are certain certainties and a lot of uncertainties. The certainties are taxes and death. Although taxes can be minimized and skipped altogether, there is no getting around death. That is a certainty for sure.

I want to share, again, the principle of the path that simply states the path you are on in life—be it financial, health, studies, marriage, relationships, etc.—will lead you to where the path goes and not necessarily where you want to be. For example, you want to do well with your studies this year, but you fail to daily put in the required amount of work. You like to go partying instead of studying, so come the time of the exams, you have to push and cram in order to get through the work. Getting a result that is less than satisfactory is no big surprise! Or perhaps you want to get rid of those few extra pounds you packed on over the past few years. Getting up early to train is hard, while eating the right foods in the right amounts is even harder (that's me), so you don't get leaner and your body does not function better. Even though it was your best intention to get it—no, *whip* it into shape—you fail miserably.

We need to remember that getting into shape is a process. When we remain focused on the process, the end result will take care of itself. Besides, it has taken us years to get into a state of "out of shape," so we cannot expect to get into shape in two weeks or four weeks or eight weeks. Follow the process and remain committed ... which seems to be the problem.

We need to remember that the principle of the path is in operation in our lives daily: the path we are on will lead us to where the path goes.

The Healing Process

> ***"And we know that all matters work together for good to those who love Elohim, to those who are called***

according to his purpose" (Romans 8:28).

We now have been through the processes as described in the book and have applied ourselves to them. We have asked, fasted and prayed, and sought the divine intervention of the Spirit of Elohim. The problem has been revealed, and we have done all that is required of us to become whole during this process. But we are possibly a little frustrated at the pace of the healing or restoration process. We might become a little discouraged while waiting for the healing to take place. This stage is where the process gets challenging.

For some of us, patience might be the easy part. For others, it is quite a challenge. Patience is required in this healing process, but it is not the only thing. We need to understand the process and how it works so that we are not disappointed and our hearts do not become sick when the hope or expectation we have is not met. Sometimes Elohim will heal instantaneously; other times the healing will take a while in order to be complete.

The beginning of this process always starts with pressure (suffering), for without pressure we will never progress to endurance (perseverance), and from endurance (perseverance) to approvedness (character) to hope (see Romans 5:3-4). Why do we have to suffer first? It is not because Elohim wants to let us suffer but rather because we "count it all joy" when we "fall into various trials, knowing that the proving of your belief works endurance. And let endurance have a perfect work, so that you be perfect and complete, lacking in naught" (James 1:2-4). So, we are to "count it all joy," which is the first step in the healing process because "the joy of Elohim is your strength" (Nehemiah 8:10). Without strength, we are weak and vulnerable to the attacks of the devil. So we must have joy—it is essential to the battle we will wage in the healing process. Joy is a supernatural element given to us by the Spirit of Elohim so that we may have the strength to endure. Joy is the ability to have strength in our well-being, knowing that all is well between us and Elohim. Without joy, we will fail and fall away because we lack the strength to endure and to persevere. Joy is the beginning point of the healing process because we will know that all is well between us and Elohim

The Path of Healing

and that that the proving of our belief works endurance in us.

Joy is the beginning point of the healing process.

We need to endure, to persevere, so that we can continue till the work is done. Endurance is defined as "the fact or power of enduring an unpleasant or difficult process or situation without giving way."[7] Endurance is needed during an unpleasant or difficult process; it is not required during an easy time. Nothing of value is needed during an easy time because then it is easy to endure. Imagine having to endure great health or great wealth or great prosperity. Those things do not require endurance; only hard and difficult times do. How is perseverance defined? It is defined as steadfastness "in doing something despite difficulty or delay in achieving success."[8] Thus you can see that both endurance and perseverance are used when times are tough, not when they are easy. When we endure, we have the power to endure an unpleasant or difficult process and the power to be steadfast in the process despite difficulty or delay in achieving success. This is mind-blowing stuff because we can then understand why endurance is so important in the healing process. It simply is training so that we don't have to go through the same thing again. "If, then, the Son makes you free, you shall be free indeed" (John 8:36). We cheat when we want out. Endurance is vital because we know that the proving of our belief works endurance, and it is vital to endure so that we may be perfect and complete, lacking in nothing (see James 1:4).

These are the things we will face every time we go through tough times, but sometimes we will not go through the process because some of the elements mentioned earlier in the book, like pride, fear or anger, are not issues for us. At the same time, we have to realize that we will not be perfect and complete and will lack for everything if we don't face the process. We must decide if we want to do this once and get it done with, or if we want to continue to circle around and around the

---

[7] Microsoft Bing, s.v. "endurance," accessed June 20, 2021, https://www.bing.com/.
[8] Microsoft Bing, s.v. "perseverance," accessed June 20, 2021, https://www.bing.com/.

problem for a long while.

This reminds me of the Israelites when they were forced to leave for the promised land. Yes, they were forced to leave slavery, and they found themselves wandering in the desert for forty years. Now this is an interesting note because the actual journey would have taken them about two weeks to complete if they had simply traveled from one point to the other. However, because of their disobedience and stubbornness and unbelief, they wandered for forty years. You and I can do the same: we can be obedient and humble and expectant and go through the tough times for two weeks, or we can wander for forty years. The choice is ours. I am not saying that those are the only time frames available; I simply want to illustrate the point. The time frame for healing is up to Elohim, but being expectant and obedient is up to us.

> "The reason why many are still troubled, still seeking, still making little forward progress is because they haven't yet come to the end of themselves. We're still trying to give orders, and interfering with God's work within us." —A. W. Tozer[9]

Healing is a process that has to be followed, has to be endured and has to be allowed to run its course in order for it to be effective. We cannot bypass some steps and expect great things to happen; we cannot skip some steps and expect healing to take place. Life is sometimes like having a gaping wound that has festered and is painful. You can ignore the wound and expect it to heal itself, but chances are good that infection will set in and that it will require medical intervention at some point to deal with the problem. When infection does set in, the physician will have to clean out the wound, which is painful. But if it is not cleaned, then the infection will persist and can lead to a loss of limb, at the very least. Once the wound is cleaned, the physician will put some ointment or balm on it, usually some anti-bacterial stuff, and

---

9 "A.W. Tozer Quotes," #5, QuoteFancy, accessed May 18, 2021, https://quotefancy.com/a-w-tozer-quotes.

The Path of Healing

bandage up the wound so that the healing process can begin. It is not a magic thing that suddenly happens because the ointment is on it; rather, it is a process to be endured.

Once the process is followed, then the healing will take place and the wound will recover from the infection. Now, this does not mean that the wound is gone; there likely will be a scar. But it does mean that the infection is gone, and we will have been healed. This is life; sometimes we are wounded in life's battles and require "medical" intervention for the wounds that we have received. The wounds will not heal on their own; they will require some tending. If we don't deal with them, they will become infected and cause more problems than what we need or want. But we tend to ignore them because they hurt a lot and we want them gone. We hope they will disappear on their own, but this wish will never work because the devil knows of these wounds and will continue to infect them so that they continue to hurt us and cause us pain, to the point of death.

> *I often use an analogy when talking to married couples who are struggling through difficult times in their relationships. I ask them to picture a granite column outside the front door with a little hammer attached to it. Each day when each partner passes the column, they strike the column just once. This happens every day for years and years, and each time the column is struck, a small chip flies out. Day after day this happens without the column ever being repaired, and each time the column is hit, it is damaged. After a while, the column is hit once more, one small chip is dislodged, and the whole column comes falling down, destroyed forever, never to be repaired again. This is how damage happens in our lives; the devil will allow us to chip away at our lives, our relationships and everything else that is important to the point that, one day, it will fall over, damaged beyond human repair. Notice I say here "human repair," for with Elohim,*

> *all things are possible (see Mark 10:27). We will be unable to repair the damage, but Elohim is able do to all things that are impossible for us.*

> "What then are we to do about our problems? We must learn to live with them until such time as God delivers us from them … We must pray for grace to endure them without murmuring. Problems patiently endured will work our spiritual perfecting. They harm us only when we resist or endure them unwillingly." – A.W. Tozer[10]

Suicide

Here is where it gets real for me because I read that suicide is the second largest cause of death in the world. I am convinced that most of these suicides are caused by some form of pain or another, by some form of mental affliction that cannot be cured by medicine. People are in emotional anguish because of depression, and if there was a known cure, then we would be able to reduce the number of deaths as a result. The devil, though, is a coward and will inflict this pain on people to drive them to death. He, the devil, infects us with a vile, evil virus that will eventually kill us if we allow it to, but there is a cure! There is a way for us to endure through the pain to healing, if we only expect that the great Elohim will be faithful to us and heal us according to His Word. We have to deal with the pain and hurt that we have experienced and allow the great physician, Elohim, to heal us and care for our wounds; we have to do our part for the healing process to happen.

If we labor and are weary, then we are commanded to come to Him, and He shall give us rest (see Matthew 11:28). You see, we are commanded to go to the very One who has put us together and who knows us, the One who died on the cross for us so that we may live; then, and only then, will we be given rest. But we often want the physician to come to us because we are tired and want to be healed on our terms. That is not how it works; we are to do it all on His terms

---

10 A.W. Tozer, quote, Idlehearts, accessed May 18, 2021, https://www.idlehearts.com/2686206/what-then-are-we-to-do-about-our-problems-we-must-learn.

and His terms only. Our obedience to His Word is driven by our love for Him; if we are disobedient, then we need to question our love and make every effort to increase it, as a fruit of the Spirit, in our lives. The more I worked on this book, the more I was convinced that this is where the crux of the matter is. Love is the driver of our wholeness and our daily walk with Elohim.

Wound Dressed
So, during the time of healing, the wound is dressed daily. That means that the dressing is removed, the wound is cleaned and inspected, and more ointment or balm is put on the wound. This dressing is done regularly so that the healing process is not disturbed and that a new infection does not occur. Removing the dressing is often painful, especially at first, as the bandage sticks to the wound and has to be removed in order to access the injury. Likewise, in our inner healing process, we have to tend to the wounds that are healing; we have to cleanse them and dress them daily to ensure that the infection does not return and healing is taking place. It is true that every time we remove the dressing we experience pain, but we are also ensuring that healing is taking place. We cleanse and tend to the wound and dress it again. This is similar to the process of tending to a young seed; it is nurtured and looked after daily so that it can grow and develop into a healthy young tree that bears good fruit in season. For a wound, we tend to it and dress it daily and in due season it will be healed and will no longer bother us.

> *This type of wound happened between my brother and I. He had stopped speaking to me because of choices I had made, and we had yet another falling out. To be clear, we did not have a good relationship anyway because of bad choices I had made earlier in my life, and at that time it did not bother me because I was spiritually dead. This time was different because I had committed my life to Elohim again and was in the church. There was a woman working in the ministry that my brother was running, and she and I*

decided to start a relationship. Today, she and I have been married for almost twenty years. However, back then the church, including my brother, was opposed to our relationship. This led to all sorts of things, and I eventually left the church. My leaving caused a bigger rift between my brother and I. Now, the rift was already there because it had not been dealt with earlier at all. The wound had been covered but not dealt with, which is an important distinction. My brother stopped talking to me, and I was really angry at him for a number of things. Unforgiveness took root in me, but fortunately I started dealing with it. Every time something happened to remind me of the unforgiveness, I would speak forgiveness over him, phone him, tell him what happened, and ask him to forgive me for my unforgiveness. This happened a few times, but eventully it started getting less frequent and less painful as I continued. I eventually stopped having to call and ask for forgiveness after about four years. That was the process, and it took that long not because I was disobedient, but because I needed to learn many things over that period of time. I endured and followed the prompting of the Spirit of Elohim every time I was told to do something, and the end result is that I was made whole and complete and lacking in nothing in this area, as James 1:4 says. I am recounting this story to illustrate that healing is a process, that the length of the process is determined by Elohim, not by us, and that we are to be obedient to the prompting of the Spirit of Elohim—so that we may be made whole and complete and lacking in nothing.

All of this needs to be driven by one thing, and one thing only, and that is our love for Elohim. If we have not love, we are like noisy brass and clanging cymbals and have nothing (see 1 Corinthians 13:1).

Afflictions and Wounds

Dealing with the emotional afflictions and wounds that we receive along the way are no different to how we deal with natural ones. We end up in battles that we have chosen or that are chosen for us and get wounded during these battles. We bleed and get infected with all sorts of nastiness; we pick up viruses and other "dis-eases" along the way and most of the time try to ignore them, gloss over them and cover them in the hope that they disappear from our lives. Sometimes we even feed and tend to them and make them grow into sizeable monsters that consume us from the inside, then wonder why we are being destroyed, why nothing is going well, and why our lives are falling apart. We need to understand that a war is going on inside us and that the victor will be the one we are obedient to. We are slaves to the one we are obedient to, it says in the Word of Elohim (see Romans 6:16). By this stage we ought to know that and believe it. Neither can we serve two masters; we will either "hate the one and love the other, or else [we] shall cleave to the one and despise the other" (Matthew 6:24). We must deal with what we have done or with what others have done to us. At this point I want to say categorically that I understand others are sometimes responsible for what has been done to us—I get it—but we are always responsible for how we respond or react to what has been done to us. If people have wronged us, then they are responsible for the act that they did, but we are responsible for what we do when we are wronged. When we react to a hurt, we are doing so in emotion. When we respond, though, we are acting in love. Remember, when Yeshua was hanging on the cross, He said, "Father, forgive them, for they do not know what they do" (Luke 23:34). I am always astounded by this statement as I think that they did know, but since Yeshua said so, I choose to believe that they did not. Even with us, when we choose to believe the Word of Elohim, then we must believe that these people who hurt us did not know what they were doing.

> *Proof of this not knowing comes from when I was growing up and my parents did things that I thought were pretty useless. Those actions probably*

> *were useless, but my parents were doing what they thought best based on their knowledge and the application of their knowledge. Today, they probably would agree that those things were pretty useless, but hindsight is always a great science. We see this in the change that happens when parents become grandparents and the "rules" change.*

So, we can believe that those who hurt us did so either intentionally or unintentionally, but we still have the responsibility of how we react or respond. If we love Elohim, then our choice is to respond, in love, to these people and to forgive them, not because they deserve forgiveness but because we love Elohim and want to be obedient to His commands. You and I have never deserved to be forgiven for our sins, for Yeshua to be sent to die on the cross for us, yet it was done. How much more, then, do we need to forgive those who sinned against us? We have a choice to make, either life or death, there is nothing else. If we are to be healed and begin this healing process, then we must choose life and choose life in abundance.

When we have learned to suffer and suffer willingly, then we will progress to the endurance part. Remember, as referenced earlier, endurance is defined as the "power of enduring an unpleasant or difficult process or situation without giving way." This means that in the suffering, when we don't quit, we have the power to go through a difficult situation or process without giving way. We don't back down and we don't give up. We face the situation and push through to the end in order to achieve victory. Think of it like having surgery.

> *When I had my neck operated on many years ago, I was bedridden for six weeks. I spent most of my time flat on my back. I got up a few times a day to move around a little and perform my ablutions, but for the rest of the time I was in bed, recovering. The pain was not that bad; it was the inability to move that got to me. I had to remain still for long periods of time, which was a test of my patience. I*

was not allowed to go anywhere in a car for the first six weeks. It was necessary for me to endure this difficult situation because it was beneficial for my health and recovery. If I did not lie still or remain at home, then I could have damaged my neck even further and jeopardized my health. This is how life is: we sometimes require surgery to remove or fix the problem and then need to convalesce or recuperate from the surgery. This convalescence is vital to the restoration process.

It is the same when we undergo spiritual "surgery"; we need to be restored to the fullness of His creation.

"And the Elohim of all favour, who called you to His everlasting esteem by Messiah Yeshua, after you have suffered a while, Himself perfect, establish, strengthen, and settle you" (1 Peter 5:10).

When we "have suffered a while," He Himself, being perfect, will "establish, strengthen and settle" us. So, we will suffer a little while; it is an integral part of the healing process. I want to stress this fact enough so that you understand how and why it is going to happen.

Restoration and Restitution
There is another concept in the healing process that we need to understand. This is the concept of restoration and restitution. We have spoken of restoration before; it is the process of being put back together again to the original condition.

Imagine a man driving through a neighborhood and spotting an old car in somebody's backyard. He stops and talks to the owner of the car and eventually negotiates a price to buy the damaged car that, although it has great value, has fallen into disrepair over the years due to neglect and abuse. The man who bought the car knows and understands its value, even though that value is not evident to anyone else. So, he buys the car, sources the parts for the restoration of the car, painstakingly

EMOTIONAL WHOLENESS

strips the car, and makes sure everything is in the condition it should be, just as it was when it was first built. The restorer might even find more damage when all the previous paint and other additions have been removed; that damage also will have to be fixed before the restoration can continue. So all the layers are stripped and all the flaws and damage exposed not to embarrass the previous owner, but to enable the restorer to identify problems that need to be fixed so as to restore the car to its former glory. Notice here that these are not cosmetic touches, but structural issues that need to be addressed. The same goes for us; we, too, are to be stripped down to the very foundation of our being so that the "structural damage" can be dealt with. The foundational framework needs to restored; we don't just do the cosmetic touch-ups and think all is well. Lastly, once the physical and mechanical restoration is done, there is one more important thing that needs to be addressed before the job is completely finished: rewiring. Rewiring is important to the whole process because without it there will not be any power and the vehicle will not run at all, despite the body work and the great engine in it.

Great body work and a good engine are nothing without rewiring.

You see, rewiring allows the whole unit to function as it should because without the electric current the vehicle will not run. If the wiring is faulty or broken, then the engine will misfire or not fire at all. If the battery is drained, then there will not be enough power to get the motor running. Similarly, we want to make sure that our structural component is sound, which is our body. It is a good thing to keep our body in shape and healthy because damage can occur when we fail to take care of it well. We also ensure that it looks good because that implies we have a great vehicle. When we fail to look after the electrical system, though, the whole vehicle can be stranded, since it would not operate the way it should. This rewiring, for us, is the change of thinking that we are commanded to do in Romans 12:2. So often we fail to change our wiring, then wonder why we are misfiring or don't "run" efficiently. We need to be rewired and plugged in to the best battery power, the Spirit of Elohim, who gives us all the power "we need for life and reverence, through the knowledge of Him" (2 Peter 1:3). Without that power, we will fail miserably and not operate the way we were intended. The rewiring is a vital step that we often overlook or miss, but it completes the process or restoration.

The restorer is also a patient person, one who understands that endurance is required to complete the task that has been undertaken, that sourcing the parts is going to be a challenge, and that the process of stripping away the layers will reveal what needs to be done. The necessary parts for this process have to be found or made, depending on availability, but once all the parts have been obtained, the restorer can begin the process of putting the car together and return it to its former glory, as if it was brand-new. This, in a nutshell, is restoration: the car is bought for a price, restored for a price and has a new owner. And this is how we are restored. We are bought for a price, which was paid on the cross. We are stripped of every bit of damage that we have incurred in life, be it abuse, rejection, emotional trauma or whatever it is; it is exposed or revealed by the restorer so that we can be made whole and repaired structurally in order for us to be the way we were designed to be.

The next part of this concept is restitution. This is where things get very interesting; you see, the process of restitution is the same as restoration, except for one major thing. The car or object, once it has been restored, will be returned to its rightful owner at no cost. Think about this for a moment.

> *Suppose someone goes out and buys a valuable object at his own expense, then pays more money to get the object restored to its former, perfect condition, expending loads of time getting the work done, only to give the object back to the rightful owner, at no cost to the previous owner.*

We must understand the enormity of this process. We have been bought with a price; we have been restored, at the great cost of the death of Yeshua on the cross; and we have been given back to our rightful owner, Yahweh our Elohim. Once we understand this process, we have really grasped the concept and so have no problem going through the restoration process. We will have no problem in suffering through the stripping process, for we know we can get rid of the damage that accumulated over our lives. We will have no problem in enduring the process until the end so that we can be made whole and complete and lacking in nothing (see James 1:4). Through Yeshua we have been restored to the original specifications of our Creator Elohim, and then we have been given back to the Creator Himself. This is what restitution does. We were bought for a price, restored to our original condition, and then returned to Yahweh through Yeshua. That is quite something to grasp and understand. We have not had to do the restoration ourselves; our only part is being obedient to the Master Craftsman who is doing the work in us and through us, and we would do well to get to the end of ourselves so that the work being done in us can be completed.

Emotions

As a side note, we, as humans, tend to connect thoughts to emotions. That means we attach our thinking to previously placed emotions and react according to that. Think of the woman who was told by Elohim that He does not like "mommies and daddies" either. Her emotions were attached to her thoughts so that whenever she was reminded of "mommies and daddies," it invoked a really bad memory for her. Each of us has had a similar experience with something in our lives where we have been hurt or damaged and every time we are reminded of that hurt, we have an adverse reaction. It is because we have tied our thoughts to our emotions.

Yeshua has set the prime example of how to dissociate our thoughts from our emotions through many stories in the Word of Elohim. For example, the man lying at the pool in John 5 had been sick for thirty-eight years. When Yeshua saw the man, He asked him if he wanted to become well. The sick man replied:

> *"Master, I have no man to put me into the pool when the water is stirred, but while I am coming, another*

steps down before me" (John 5:7).

You see, the man tied his thoughts with his emotions. Instead of answering the question, he went into some sort of emotional retort about why he never gets the chance. Yeshua did not ask him why he was not well, but because of all the emotional baggage, his response to Yeshua was based on his feelings rather than his thought process. The sick man needed to be rewired; he needed to redo his thinking. Yeshua immediately responded with, "Rise, take up your bed and walk" (John 5:8). Here is a prime example of not tying thoughts to emotions. I am convinced that Yeshua could have said something like, "I am really sorry to hear of your predicament. I understand how you feel, but let's get this sorted out." No, the simple response, based on His pure thought, is to rise up, take the bed and go home. I love that Yeshua is so blunt in His approach; He knows the value of thought over emotion and how to disconnect His thoughts from His emotions—something that most people have failed to grasp and master.

Yeshua's Temptation
Another of my favorite examples is when Yeshua is led into the wilderness for forty days and nights to be tempted by the devil. After this time, He was tired and hungry, and the devil came to Him and said:

> *"If You are the Son of Elohim, command that these stones become bread" (Matthew 4:3).*

Yeshua could have done that without a fuss, but He did not allow His emotions to rule His actions. Instead, His thoughts led Him back to the Word of Elohim and all He did was quote the truth. This is, by far, the best example of disconnecting thought from emotion. That does not mean Yeshua was not hungry; rather, it meant that He did not allow His emotions to rule His thoughts. We, as people in need of restoration, must learn to disconnect our thoughts from our emotions so that we can operate in the power of the Spirit of Elohim and not in our fleshly desires. We need to be rewired by the very Restorer who has knit us together in our mother's womb. As the Word of Elohim says:

> *"For the rest, brothers, whatever is true, whatever is noble, whatever is righteous, whatever is clean, whatever is lovely, whatever is of good report, if there is any uprightness and if there is any praise – think on these" (Philippians 4:8).*

This is what happens when we disconnect emotion from thought. We allow ourselves to dwell on the Word of Elohim, thereby transforming our minds and not conforming to the patterns of the world (see Romans 12:2). We allow the Word of Elohim to permeate our thinking to the point that our thoughts of what is true and noble override the world standard of how we feel. This does not mean that the emotions no longer exist; instead, it means that we believe in what is written in the Word of Elohim before we believe in the way we feel or the way things make us feel. The current world standard is that our feelings are important and take preference over truth. This is contrary to the Word of Elohim, and we should never conform to the patterns of the world. Disconnecting our thoughts from our emotions simply means that we believe in the truth before we believe in our feelings. This way of thinking does not come easy; it is a hard-fought-for thing, and we need to be intentional in pursuing it. This transformation will not happen on its own.

> *I heard the story of a young married man who had to deal with a very tough situation in his marriage. His wife at the time had had an affair, which he suspected she had done, and when this truth was finally revealed, it came with one more little surprise: she had gotten pregnant as a result of this affair. During the three months leading up to the exposure of the truth, this man had fasted and prayed and sought the specific desire of Elohim. When everything finally came out, he was not at all upset about the affair because he had decided to trust in Elohim and in the power of His Spirit. He had disconnected*

his feelings from his thoughts. It would have been easy to feel aggrieved or to feel done in by what had happened, but he decided to put his trust in Elohim. Her having an affair really hurt him, but he had decided that he was going to respond in love rather than react to how he felt. Because he had disconnected his feelings from his thoughts, he could deal with the situation according to the Word of Elohim. He was able to operate in the power of the Word of Elohim and not in the power of his feelings.

As it is written in Ephesians 4:26:

"'Be wroth [angry], but do not sin.' Do not let the sun go down on your rage."

This verse implies that we are allowed to be angry, that we are allowed to have an emotion, but we are not to sin or to fall prey to the emotion. Yeshua Himself displayed anger when He drove the moneychangers and other vendors out of the temple (see John 2:13-16). I am convinced that He was angry when He did so, but He did not sin. We are allowed to have emotions, but we would do well to disconnect them from our thoughts so that we do not sin.

We need to expect that we will be made whole and complete without any evidence being seen; that is the crux of belief. But we want to be whole and complete before getting on with life. When things are right, we will step out and get things done; we need everything to be perfect before we move forward. However, remember, as Mark Batterson said, that Elohim does not always call the qualified, but He always qualifies the called. Belief means that we set out on this journey with the expectation that we will be restored to our former, whole selves while not having any evidence of the end result. We need this belief to be based on our love for Elohim and nothing else.

Imagine, if you will, being called to go and walk around a walled city once a day for six days, carrying the ark of the covenant and playing the trumpet. (See Joshua 6.) Now, as a soldier, I know that this action will not get the job done of capturing a city or of defeating the enemy. But Yahweh, in His infinite wisdom, had other plans, like He usually does. On the seventh day, the Israelites were to march around the city walls seven times. At the order of Joshua, they were to roar, and the walls would fall down. Once again, as a soldier, I can see the obvious flaw here, but Yahweh knows much better than I do and is an infinitely better tactician than me. The proof is there that, at the roar, the walls of Jericho fell flat, and the Israelites gained the victory they were promised. So when the Spirit of Elohim prompts us to do something that makes no sense, we should heed the call and do it, even if we see no evidence of anything happening, and especially if we see nothing happening. Our belief is the substance of what is being expected even though we have not yet seen it. Think of Yeshua, who in John 9 healed the blind man by making mud with His spit and then putting it on the man's eyes. None of that makes sense to us, but it never has to; we just need to be expectant and obedient.

A.W. Tozer summed this up extremely well:

> "True faith rests upon the character of God and asks no further proof than the moral perfections of the One who cannot lie." —A.W. Tozer[11]

This is the essence of the healing process: we expect healing and require no proof except that we believe in the character of Elohim.

Once the process of healing has started, we are to stay the course until the healing is complete. We have to repeat this process for every bit of healing that is required. Just as a car undergoes various processes in its restoration, so do we. There is no one thing that fixes all type of wounds or hurts. I am sorry if this disappoints you, but we all will go through the process regularly. The Word commands us so when Yeshua says in Luke 9:23, "If anyone wishes to come after Me, let him deny himself, and take up his stake daily, and follow Me." This is not a once-off thing; it is something that is done every day. There is no

---

11 "A.W. Tozer Quotes," #17, QuoteFancy, accessed May 19, 2021, https://quotefancy.com/a-w-tozer-quotes.

difference between this command and forgiving others or sowing and reaping, for example. We follow Him daily, as long as today is today. But, you may ask, why is this a process? Why can it not be done in a second and be over? Well, nothing says it cannot happen that way, but the timing will be according to the will of the Spirit of Elohim, just as it is written that the Spirit of Elohim works all of the gifts, "distributing to each one individually as He intends" (1 Corinthians 12:11). Healing is a gift that we receive, and that healing will take place as the Spirit of Elohim intends.

I have witnessed many times the instantaneous healing of people as well as the healing over time. I can only speculate that for some people there were other things that the Spirit needed to deal with before healing would take place. The point here is that we need to press on and in to a closer relationship with the Almighty Elohim so that we can enjoy the satisfaction of His presence, for in His "presence is joy to satisfaction" (Psalm 16:11). There is no clear answer to the difference in healing, but I do know that we are all on a path to wholeness and that each of us is treated differently and have to do some things differently. The end result, however, is always the same. We will never be tried above that which we can handle, and there will always be a way of escape, enabling us to bear it, as the Spirit of Elohim intends (see 1 Corinthians 10:13).

> *Take, for example, the well-known story of Joni Eareckson Tada who was paralyzed from the neck down in a diving accident when she was seventeen years old. Joni had expected Elohim to heal her, but He had other plans, and so she had to contend with her circumstances. She explains in her story that she had to work hard to get out of the cycle of depression—and that is what was done by her thinking, and then doing what was thought of.*[12]

It is easy to read the Word of Elohim, but it is entirely a different

---

[12] "Joni Eareckson Tada Story: Joni's Story - Page 1," Life Story (website), accessed June 20, 2021, joniearecksontadastory/jonis-story-page-1/.

thing to do the words.

Joni Eareckson Tada's story is extremely inspiring. If you are battling with your thinking, reading her story should help you in your battle. The big question is why did Elohim not heal her? Why did He allow her to remain in this situation? When we see that her story has helped countless others in their struggles, then we begin to understand the intention of Elohim. We will never be able to fully comprehend the magnitude of Elohim or His plans, but I have come to the realization that He is sovereign, and His wisdom is supreme.

Understanding this truth is the big challenge we have when facing our problems.

Chapter Nine
The Process of Wholeness

Wholeness Process

As for the process of wholeness, remember that there is a process and that a process, as mentioned earlier, is defined as "a series of actions or steps taken in" a certain sequence to achieve a certain end.[1] Wholeness is a process, a series of actions or steps taken in a certain order to achieve wholeness in a certain area. This process can be likened to baking a cake, in which there are a number of ingredients involved that are used to get to an end result. These ingredients need to be blended and added in a certain way and then baked for a certain amount of time to get the cake. Imagine if you got the wrong ingredients or mixed them in the wrong sequence. You would not get the desired result! The cake would flop or not set properly and would be inedible.

The wholeness process is similar; we need to do or not do things in a set sequence for a certain time, and when we do not do things properly, then it goes wrong and we get upset at the result. We cannot do the same thing over and over and expect that we are going to get a different result each time. We need to change the recipe or change the ingredients if we are to get different results. Our thinking has to change

---

[1] Microsoft Bing, s.v. "process" accessed June 15, 2021.

before we undertake this journey. We need to accept responsibility for our own selves instead of blaming others for the predicament we are in. We need a new recipe that has been tried and tested by the Master who knows that it will not fail or flop. This "recipe" has been used thousands of times and is the same yesterday, today and forevermore.

We cannot perfect the works of Elohim; He is the perfection that we need. We must emulate His example if we are to have any chance of healing and wholeness in our lives. We must work hard to stop arrogance and pride from getting in the way of the restoration in our lives. If we don't, we will mix up the order of the recipe and cause all sorts of chaos in our lives, then wonder why we have not been restored and made whole. This work is not an easy task; it is not for the faint of heart; it is a tiresome and meticulous project that requires endurance and grit and that we push through to the end. But we are weak and tired and heavy laden. We have had no rest, so we become dogged down by life to the point of exhaustion—physical, mental and spiritual. This scenario only happens because we don't follow the recipe set out for us in the Word of Elohim. We deviated from the process or added other ingredients or left out key ingredients because we think we know better or that others, not Elohim, have the secret to success.

Doing so makes no sense as it would be like telling a pro golfer how to make a shot, how to swing the club, or how to win a tournament, without ever having played golf ourselves. This is pure arrogance and pride in action. We need to get back to the position of humility where we declare that we are "awesomely and wondrously made" (Psalm 139:14) by a very great and awesome Creator who knows exactly how we are made and what needs to be fixed. In other words, we need to defer to the Creator who knows the recipe for success.

The Word sums it up perfectly when it says:

> *"For from within, out of the heart of men, proceed evil reasonings, adulteries, whorings, murders, thefts, greedy desires, wickedness, deceit, indecency, an evil eye, blasphemy, pride, foolishness. All these wicked matters come from within and defile a man" (Mark 7:21-23).*

This is quite a summary. This passage clearly sums up how we think as people—"There is none righteous, no, not one!" (Romans 3:10)—but we want to argue with the truth of Elohim. We think we know better, then we become stressed and depressed when things don't go well for us. Is it any wonder? It is further written:

"Do not be led astray: Elohim is not mocked, for whatever a man sows, that he shall also reap. Because he who sows to his own flesh shall reap corruption from the flesh, but he who sows to the Spirit shall reap everlasting life from the Spirit" **(Galatians 6:7-8).**

But here is the kicker, the very essence of this passage:

"And let us not lose heart in doing good, for in due season we shall reap if we do not grow weary" **(Galatians 6:9).**

We are not to lose heart; we are to endure. We are to stand fast and push through our difficult times without giving way so that we may reap what we have sown.

Why is all of this so important in the wholeness process, you may ask? Because the hardest part to deal with in the wholeness process might be the time of waiting and restoration. We are impatient and live in a world of instantaneous gratification. We want stuff, and we want it now. There is no more patience for things to happen, and we become discouraged or impatient when things don't happen at our pace.

The body has an amazing ability to heal itself, which in itself is the work of the Creator of heaven and earth. Yahweh Himself created us so that we are able to heal; however, we have corrupted the system by the foods we eat and the lifestyles we live. We have destroyed our body's ability to heal itself because we have sown destruction into our mortal flesh for our whole lives. We reap what we sow. This is also true for our mental health. We have sown years and years of death and then wonder why we have fallen into disrepair in this area. We should not wonder but should know that we have done immense damage to ourselves and that we are responsible for what we have done to ourselves. At the same time, we also should know that there is a hope of healing, there is a chance for us to be restored back to health and be made whole again. We must renew our thinking on the wholeness of our life, both spiritually and emotionally, so that we can be healed and possess life—and "possess it beyond measure," as we have been promised (John 10:10).

There is always a hope of healing.

Now, possessing life "beyond measure" does not mean that we will be financially well off, have a great job or career, or drive a great car; it means that we will be able to live the life we have been called to by Elohim, and live that life "beyond measure." Think of Yeshua. He is the Son of the Most High Elohim and was called to earth, but He did not have an extravagant lifestyle; He did not have custom-made robes or fancy horses. As a matter of fact, He was so broke that He had to borrow a donkey's colt to ride into Jerusalem (see Matthew 21). Here is Yeshua, the Messiah, riding into a city on a borrowed donkey. This incident does not speak of any stature whatsoever, but He was the Messiah, and He truly lived and possessed life and life "beyond measure." We need to start understanding that life "beyond measure" is defined by Elohim and not by man or by the world's standard.

Becoming whole is a process we have to endure. It is to be suffered with humility, with joy and without murmuring so that the Great Physician can do His work in us. This requires that we understand the process and allow ourselves to go through it with joy. There are a few important ingredients that we need to understand so that we can go through it. These ingredients include, but are not limited to, patience, rehabilitation, preparation, planning, execution, belief, obedience and rest.

Patience

In order for us to be able to rest, we will need patience. We are too highly strung. We want to see immediate results; we want instant gratification and deliverance from our problems and afflictions; but that is not always going to happen. Yahweh will decide what the best way is, and we are to trust in Him, period, not for something but just in Him. We need to trust in Him and then be patient while waiting for the thing that we are expecting. Patience is a fruit of the Spirit of Elohim, one that we need if we are to endure the healing process and become whole. Remember that patience is not the ability to wait, but the attitude we display while we are waiting, as Joyce Meyer said in *Battlefield of the Mind*. We are like a farmer who goes through the process of preparing his land for his crop and after planting his crop patiently waits for the harvest. This does not mean that he remains inactive; rather, it means he exercises patience while waiting for the growing process to happen.

Rehabilitation

Part of the healing process is rehabilitation. One way to define rehabilitation is as "the action of restoring something that has been damaged to its former condition."[2] For example, when a prized piece of land is destroyed by fire, it is rehabilitated to its former condition. What is interesting to note here is that the land does not restore itself but is helped by an outside force until it can take care of itself. When a fire has damaged the land, new seeds have to be planted by an outside force—for example, birds or other animals—so that the vegetation may grow and populate the land. In order for the seed to grow, the soil has to be prepared. You and I need this rehabilitation in our life; we need for our soil, which is our minds, to be prepared so that the new seed will take root and grow. The better prepared the soil is, the better the seed will grow. We must understand that our minds are either fertile or infertile ground and

---

2 Microsoft Bing, s.v. "rehabilitation," accessed June 20, 2021, https://www.bing.com/.

that what we sow in them will either flourish or be overtaken by weeds and die. We are responsible for the rehabilitation of the soil of our minds by the washing of the Word of Elohim, which means that we must meditate on the Word day and night and allow ourselves to be transformed in our thinking by this meditation (see Ephesians 5:26; Joshua 1:8; Romans 12:2). Allowing the Word to transform us is how we till the soil to be fertile and ready for the seeds of the Spirit of Elohim to be planted in.

Preparation

We are to prepare ourselves for the season of restoration and healing because without preparation we are doomed to failure. In the military we had a saying about "the rule of P": "Proper planning prevents pretty poor performance." This saying means that we must plan properly in order to achieve an expected outcome, but also know that a plan is a basis for change. In other words, we must know that once we are in battle, we will have to think and assess while we engage the enemy. Fortunately for us, the thinking process has been predetermined according to the Word of Elohim and we only have to execute the plan given to us. So, our planning is to execute the plan of Elohim by being watchful, by being vigilant and by putting on the full armor of Elohim, knowing that:

> ***"We do not wrestle against flesh and blood, but against principalities, against authorities, against the world-rulers of the darkness of this age, against spiritual matters of wickedness in the heavenlies" (Ephesians 6:12).***

This is a huge deal! We should be prepared to combat the evil one who is hell-bent on coming "to steal, and to slaughter, and to destroy" (John 10:10).

Planning

We are required to plan our steps and then submit those steps to Elohim, who will establish them according to His desire and His

The Process of Wholeness

purpose (see Proverbs 16:3). We often want to plan our own thing and then are miserable when our plans fail, all because we did not submit them for approval by the Supreme Commander of the universe. Elohim has a plan for each and every one of us, "plans of peace and not of evil, to give you a future and an expectancy" (Jeremiah 29:11). We are required to plan and then to submit it for approval, but we often go it alone—with disastrous results. In any military operation the commander executing the plan is responsible for the planning, and he will always submit his planning to his superior officer for approval. I believe that, in the unseen war that we are involved in, we should always submit our planning to Elohim for approval. Then we are expected to succeed.

Execution

Once the planning is complete, we are to execute the plan that was made. This execution is often violent in nature and usually not what we expect it to be. Consider the Israelites who were marching around Jericho in Joshua chapter 6. For six days nothing happened. That does not seem to fit into the battle plan because walking around a city does not destroy it. On the seventh day they walked around the city seven times, and on the seventh time around they were to shout. They did, and the walls came tumbling down. As a military practitioner, I am amazed at the awesomeness of Elohim's military prowess, which is far superior to mine. My belief and trust is in Him, and in Him alone, and I have always maintained that we are to execute the plan with utmost discipline and obedience so that the authority and power of Elohim are exalted.

Belief

We are to believe that Elohim is omnipotent and supreme in every way. We are to believe that His "'thoughts are not your thoughts, neither are your ways My ways,' declares יהוה" (Isaiah 55:8). This is the heart of the matter: that we believe in Elohim, that we know that "without belief it is impossible to please Him, for he who comes to Elohim has to believe that He is, and that He is a rewarder of those who earnestly seek Him" (Hebrews 11:6).

Our belief is that He *is* ... not that He is good or kind or lovely, but that He *is*. This is awesome, and when we get to that point, then we know that we are on the right track. We need to read Hebrews 11 again to get a full understanding of what belief looks like. Our belief is the very crux of the whole matter of wholeness, and it will lead us to earnestly seek Him.

> "FAITH [belief] means Forwarding All Issues To Heaven" –Anonymous

Obedience

One of the key elements to healing is obedience. When we obey, when we do as commanded, then we operate in the authority and power of the Word of Elohim. According to D.L. Moody, "There will be no peace in any soul until it is obedient to the voice of God."[3] So, being obedient means that we will have peace, "the peace of Elohim, which surpasses all understanding" (Philippians 4:7), and true belief will manifest itself in the performance of works of obedience. It is interesting to note the meaning of the word as used in the New and Old Testaments. In the Old Testament, the Hebrew words *shama`* and *hupakoe* are frequently translated as to obey and to listen in a position of submission, respectively."[4] The words carry an underlying tone of reverence and obedience, of subordination as a soldier ranking under an officer. In the New Testament we also have the word *peitho,* which means "obey, yield to, comply with" and to trust in, to believe in.[5] Obedience is essential for our healing.

Rest

We are required to rest when we are healing.

> *"Come to Me, all you who labour and are burdened, and I shall give you rest" (Matthew 11:28).*

---

[3] "D.L. Moody Quotes," #13, QuoteFancy, accessed May 19, 2021, https://quotefancy.com/d-l-moody-quotes.
[4] *The NAS Old Testament Hebrew Lexicon*, s.v. "shama'," accessed June 20, 2021, https://www.biblestudytools.com/lexicons/hebrew/nas/shama.html and *The KJV New Testament Greek Lexicon*, s.v. "hupakoe," accessed June 20, 2021, https://www.biblestudytools.com/lexicons/greek/kjv/hupakoe.html.
[5] *The KJV New Testament Greek Lexicon*, s.v. "peitho," accessed June 20, 2021, https://www.biblestudytools.com/lexicons/greek/kjv/peitho.html.

This is not a physical rest, although one of the benefits of this rest is that we will physically be more at rest than before; but it is a spiritual rest that allows us to be at peace in a world full of turmoil. The effects of anxiety and stress on our bodies is that we may experience extreme fatigue and feel excessively sluggish and lethargic to the point of exhaustion. Sleeping well only helps so much. Getting rest, though, is like ointment for our soul because it allows us to let go and stop the busyness in our mind. Is it any wonder we feel recharged after spending two weeks of vacation with our feet in the sand, or breathing in fresh air in the woods next to a large lake? We need to be able to rest, physically, but we need to rest spiritually and mentally, too. We need go to the very One who put us together and He will give us rest (see Matthew 11:28). Along with rest is recuperation, which is the restoring of one's health and power through rest. We are never to underestimate the importance of rest in the healing process. Resting means letting go of the problem, doing what we need to do, and then allowing the Spirit of Elohim to heal us where He deems necessary.

Conclusion
So, let me conclude this discussion here. The process starts with knowing that there is a problem. We need a revelation to show us that something is wrong, and this is because we have asked Yahweh to search us and know us (see Psalm 139:23). The second step is dealing with the problem, and in this step, we are to actually deal with the things that have been revealed to us in the first step. During this step, we will have everything we need to deal with what has been revealed to us; we will never be tested above what we can handle, plus there will always be a way made that allows us to deal and bear with the test (see 1 Corinthians 10:13). We also have been promised that we can do all things through Yeshua who strengthens us (see Philippians 4:13). When we have done these things, then healing will take place and we will live life, and life in abundance; we will be whole (see John 10:10). Following this process is not an easy thing to do; it is not like putting a bandage over a minor scratch and not worrying about it. It is an active choice and an intense desire to live this life. This choice needs to be fueled by love and desire, without which we will fail.

> *"As many as I love, I reprove and discipline. So be ardent and repent" (Revelation 3:19).*

As discussed earlier, *process* is defined as "a series of actions or steps taken" in a specific sequence in order to achieve a specific end. This has been one of the central subjects of this book and is clearly outlined all the way through. The underpinning cornerstone, the very life of this writing, is love—the very powerful, unfailing and glorious love of Yahweh, our Elohim, who "so loved the world that He gave His only brought-forth Son, so that everyone who believes in Him should not perish but possess everlasting life" (John 3:16). This very passage has its roots in love, and we should imprint that in our minds and in our hearts and then believe it with everything we have, for it is the very foundation of our wholeness.

When I set out to write this book, it was going to be a quick case of "reveal, deal and heal" because, in essence, this is what it actually is. But I came to the realization that my writing that would be in vain because of the lack of foundational strength and integrity. Thus, this foundation is based in and on love, nothing more and nothing less.

I am reminded of the scripture that talks about our labor. It says:

> *"Therefore, my beloved brothers, be steadfast, immovable, always excelling in the work of the Master, knowing that your labour is not in vain in the Master" (1 Corinthians 15:58).*

This verse cements the approach that we should labor in love, in the Master. We have been saved by favor, "through belief, and that not of yourselves, it is the gift of Elohim, it is not by works, so that no one should boast" (Ephesians 2:8-9). It is important that you understand that all of this discussion in this book is through Him, by Him and for Him.

We have not yet fully understood the power of the love of Elohim because if we did, then our lives would be radically altered in the best way possible. We have a very "airy fairy" understanding, based on the watered-down approach by the institution of church, which has led to a very weak "Christianity" in the modern world. This weakening happened because one of the fundamental teachings of the institution of church is that the love of Elohim is unconditional. That is one of the biggest lies ever spread because it allows modern Christians to live sinful lives and have no fear for the judgment that is to come. Let me explain this just a little.

The love of Yahweh is not unconditional, as most would say, because nowhere in the Word of Elohim does it say so. If the Word does not say it, then it does not exist. The love of Yahweh is unfailing, but never unconditional. There is a big difference between the two. The Word of Elohim says that love never fails (see 1 Corinthians 13:8), but it never says that love is unconditional. As a matter of fact, when we read chapter 13 of the first book of Corinthians, we see that it clearly sets out the boundaries for what love is. It is patient and kind and on the list goes, to end with love "covers all, believes all, expects all, endures all. Love never fails" (1 Corinthians 13:4-8).

The love of Yahweh is unfailing.

When we start to understand this with our hearts, minds and souls and truly begin to live it, then we know that love is conditional.

> *Imagine for a moment, if you will, coming home and finding your spouse in bed with someone else. How would that make you feel? I am convinced that the majority of people would have a very negative reaction to this happening, and anything similar to it. Why is it, then, that love is not unconditional? We would love them despite what they have done, right? Not so fast. We would be angry, hurt, devastated and betrayed by this scene, and rightly so. None of that will change until the guilty partner apologizes, asks for your forgiveness, and walks in that repentance, for love never fails.*

The same is true for us and Yahweh. When we sin, we are required to do something about it. First, we confess it, according to 1 John 1:9, then "He is trustworthy and righteous to forgive us the sins and cleanse us from all unrighteousness."

So, the condition for forgiveness is that we are to confess our sins, or in other words, make a formal declaration stating that we are guilty of the crime. The condition is that we confess our sins before any forgiveness can take place. The Word clearly says that "if we confess our sins He is trustworthy and righteous to forgive us the sins and cleanse us from all unrigtheousness" (1 John 1:9). Thus the condition is the confession, and this is applicable to all sin all the time. The same is true of conditional love. The Word of Elohim is clear when it says that "Elohim so loved the world that He gave His only brought-forth Son, so that everyone who believes in Him should not perish but possess everlasting life" (John 3:16). Here again is a great statement of truth and condition. "So that everyone who believes in Him" ... you see this is not a right that you and I are afforded because we go to church and "believe" in Him; even "the demons also believe—and shudder" (James 2:19). So what is the difference, then? The scriptures say that belief without works is dead (see James 2:20). That's right, this means that we can believe there is only one Elohim—and we would do well to do so—without also having the fruit that supports our belief. This means that we believe everything that is written in the Word of Elohim from the start to the end—or we believe nothing at all. Many institutions preach that the love of Elohim is unconditional, but I must warn you that that is a false teaching and those who believe it that will pay dearly.

Read Matthew 7:21 where it says, "Not everyone who says to Me, 'Master, Master,' shall enter into the reign of the heavens, but he who is doing the desire of My Father in the heavens." We read in verses 22 and 23 that there will those who say, "'Master, Master, have we not prophesied in Your Name, and cast out demons in Your Name, and done many mighty works in Your Name?' And then I shall declare to them 'I never knew you, depart from Me, you who work lawlessness!'"

Now, I am sure that this does not sound like unconditional love. If it was, then those people would have been welcomed into the fold with open arms. Furthermore, we can state that love is dependant on the condition of obedience, as in "If you love Me, you will obey My commands" (see John 14:23). You see, love is conditional, and if the conditions for love are set by Elohim, then He will not defy His own conditions. Elohim is the standard of conditional love; He is love and has therefore defined love and all its conditions as set out in His Word. Just to be clear, *conditional* means that something is subject to one or more requirements or conditions being met. This certainly is true for love, and it is true because it is written in the Word of Elohim.

I urge all of us to take a deep look at the meaning and value of love and use it as it was intended by the very One who is love, Elohim Himself. Once we have a firm grasp of this love, then our lives will be transformed by its power. Then we will be able to walk in love, as "Messiah also has loved us, and gave Himself for us, a gift and an offering to Elohim for a sweet-smelling fragrance" (Ephesians 5:2). Everything we have should be based on and in this love because it is a gift, and we should never cheapen it or diminish the act of love that sent the Messiah to the cross for us.

> *"[Love] covers all, believes all, expects all, endures all. Love never fails" (1 Corinthians 13:7-8).*

> *"And now belief, expectation, and love remain – these three. But the greatest of these is love" (1 Corinthians 13:13).*

Shalom

Chapter Ten
The Power of Action

Action Plan

So, now that we know what obstacles to look for, what do we do with them? In this chapter I am going to detail an action plan of what to do with the obstacles that stop us from becoming whole and rob us of the life that was meant for us, the life as described in John 10:10:

> *"The thief does not come except to steal, and to slaughter, and to destroy. I have come that they might possess life, and that they might possess it beyond measure" (John 10:10).*

When we are made whole and complete, we will be able to possess the life spoken of here and will be able to live as "more than overcomers" (Romans 8:37). But, in order to do this, we will need to persevere, for this road may be rocky and uneven, unnerving and long. It may be fraught with pain and tears, but in the end there will be a just reward. We need to persevere on this road so that perseverance will have its "perfect work, so that you be perfect and complete, lacking in naught" (James 1:4). Notice again the word *complete*, which means whole. Stand strong and above all else, stand (see Ephesians 6:13).

We can see from our discussions that there are a number of obstacles that will hinder our progress from brokenness to wholeness. Every one of these factors plays a vital and pivotal role in our destruction with or without our knowledge. So, if we don't know what we don't know, then how do we make any progress? How do we get from where we are to where we should be? The rest of this chapter is dedicated to unlocking the powerful healing path towards wholeness.

Step 1: Ask
Realize that you don't know what you don't know. Being unaware is not sin, but staying in that state is rather foolish, so it is best to ask. The psalmist says in Psalm 139 that Elohim has searched him and known him. It goes on to say that Elohim, who created us, who knit us together in the depths of the earth, has searched us and known us. The psalmist continues on with more of this incredible psalm, but ends with the following:

> *"Search me, O El, and know my heart; try me, and know my thoughts; and see if an idolatrous way is in me, and lead me in the way everlasting"* **(Psalm 139:23-24).**

Why would the psalmist, who has declared that Elohim has searched him and known him, be asking this again? I believe it is because we develop offensive ways through our thinking that then become the way we do things. Our thoughts lead to our actions. It is clearly written that as a man "reckons" (or thinks, or considers) in his heart, so he is (Proverbs 23:7). Our thinking is important since it shapes who we become. When we align our thinking with the thinking of the Messiah and with the Word of Elohim, then we become the men and women whom Elohim has called us to be. So, ask Elohim to search you and show you your heart. Ask Him to reveal to you whether there be any offensive ways in you that hinder your growth and your wholeness in Him.

The Power of Action

Ask Elohim to search you.

Matthew 7:7 illustrates this for us:

"Ask and it shall be given to you, seek and you will find, knock and it shall be opened for you."

We don't receive because we don't ask, and we don't ask because we are afraid of the answer. For example, have you ever cheated on your taxes? Have you ever cheated in your exams? Have you ever cheated on your spouse? There is a myriad of questions that can be asked here, but I like how the psalmist says it:

"... Try me, and know my thoughts; and see if an idolatrous way is in me" (Psalm 139:23-24).

The challenge is to be bold—to ask the question and then allow the Spirit of Elohim to reveal what needs to be done.

"And I say to you: ask and it shall be given to you, seek and you shall find, knock and it shall be opened to you. For everyone asking receives, and he who is seeking finds, and to him who is knocking it shall be opened. And what father among you whose son asks for bread shall give him a stone, or if he asks for a fish shall give him a snake instead of a fish, or if he asks for an egg shall give him a scorpion?" (Luke 11:9-12)

This discussion ends with this:

"If you then, being wicked, know how to give good gifts to your children, how much more shall your

Father from heaven give the Set-apart Spirit to those asking Him!" (Luke 11:13)

Step 2: Accept Responsibility

It is very easy to blame someone or something else for why and where you are at in life. I am reminded of the comic strip I would hand out to delinquents and addicts that depicted a boy at the psychologist's office. In the first picture frame the boy says to the psychologist, "Doc, I have been coming here for twelve sessions now, when is my life going to change?" In the second frame the psychologist answers, "When you start taking responsibility for your own life." The third and final frame goes like this: the boy is standing with his hands on his head, exasperated and says, "Why does everybody try and make my life my responsibility!"[1]

I think this comic sums it all up so well. We are quick to blame others for the condition of our lives, for the mess we are in, or for the lack of progress we have made, and we greatly dislike the idea of having to take responsibility for our own selves, for our own thoughts and actions. Yes, bad things may have happened to us, and yes, we may be bearing the scars of a past trauma, but we cannot continue to blame others for the way we are. Life is ten percent of what happens to us and ninety percent of how we respond to what happened to us, says Charles Swindoll.[2] Notice that I use the word *respond* here, not *react*. We can choose to be ten percenters, or we can choose to be ninety percenters. This does not mean that we will only ever be ninety percent, but it does means that we can choose to respond, in love, to our situations, to our hurts and traumas.

Why do we need to choose to respond? The reason is quite simple. When we react, it is almost always an emotional thing, and we allow it to rule our behavior. When we respond, on the other hand, it is out of love. Thus, taking responsibility for ourselves is a vital step in our healing. The fact that we were dealt a bad hand, were abused or were given up for adoption matters little compared to how we deal

---

[1] Bill Watterson, *Calvin and Hobbes*, syndicated from November 18, 1985 to December 31, 1995.
[2] Charles R. Swindoll, "Charles R. Swindoll Quotes," Goodreads, accessed May 23, 2021, https://www.goodreads.com/quotes/1169-life-is-10-what-happens-to-you-and-90-how.

The Power of Action

with the issues we have. When we take responsibility, we own it, can control it and can do something about it. We are always responsible for ourselves ... take that truth and own it.

Take responsibility: own your issues.

Remember the story of the two boys who grew up in foster care? The one became a stable and successful young man while the other one, who had exactly the same circumstances, became a homeless alcoholic and drug-addicted bum. You see, when you couple a repentant heart with taking responsibility, then healing can truly begin.

That story is a great example of how as a man "reckons" (or thinks, or considers) in his heart, so he is (Proverbs 23:7). Two brothers, who had shared the same past, landed up in very different situations because of thinking. Never underestimate the power of your thought life.

What process are you to follow when you are in a situation or position in life where you realize that you are not whole and that you are in need of help? What do you need to understand and do?

Understand your own responsibility.

Understand that something happened to you that you may or not have been responsible for. If you were responsible, then accept it and move forward. If you were not responsible, then accept it and move forward, too. Either way, you have to move on.

Understand that you cannot control everything in life. You can control what happens in your life, but not what happens to your life.

For example, suppose you are travelling along to work one morning and some other driver who is not paying attention drives into the back of your car. You have no control over that, but what you do next is fully in and under your control.

The only thing you have full control over is you ... always. Your thoughts, your emotions and your attitudes are all yours; you cannot ever delegate responsibility of those to someone else. During some of our arguments, my wife would say that I made her angry, and my response would be, "Great! Because if I can control your emotions, then I am going to be the happiest man in the world. Because then I can control your moods, your feelings of love, etc." We all know where this story goes after this. Accept responsibility for your life.

Obey.

Be obedient to the Spirit of Elohim and allow Him to lead you into all truth. Obedience "is better than a slaughtering [sacrifice]," as 1 Samuel 15:22 says. Obedience takes courage, and once again the Word says that we have not been given "a spirit of cowardice, but of power and of love and of self-control" (2 Timothy 1:7). You see, we need courage to be able to do things, and for this reason we have been given the spirit of power.

Execute the plan.

Then, finally, execute the plan. It is of no use if we know this stuff and do nothing with it. Knowledge is not power without the application of it. The Word says to not be hearers of the Word only, but doers of it (see James 1:22). The previous verse is an awesome qualifier. It says:

> *"Therefore put away all filthiness and overflow of evil, and receive with meekness the implanted Word, which is able to save your lives" (James 1:21).*
>
> *"I have called the heavens and the earth as witnesses today against you: I have set before you life and death, the blessing and the curse. Therefore you shall choose life, so that you live, both you and your seed" (Deuteronomy 30:19).*

Here again we have life and death put before us. The best, but by no means the easy, choice is life.

The Power of Action

The testimony of a young man, which I heard, comes to mind here. This young man battled with pornography and chose life over death in this area. Whenever he would travel, he would take a mentor with him. He would book a reservation at hotels and the first thing he would do is ask for a room without a television. He would explain to the hotel staff that he had battled with pornography and did not want to be led into temptation. If a room without a television was not available, then he would ask the hotel staff to block the television so that he would not be able to access any channels of this nature. This was quite a bold and courageous action, but it speaks volumes of a man taking responsibility for his own life and employing godly principles to stay pure.

This young man understood the power of life and death choices and had chosen life over death, blessing over curse. This action required courage and obedience, both of which are life choices. We are able to do all things "through Messiah who empowers" us (Philippians 4:13).

Let me explain about truth and fact here for a moment, just for the sake of clarity. We often use the word *truth* as in "this is the truth," but I feel that we need clarity in this area because there is fact and then there is truth. The difference between the two is that the truth remains constant. The Word of Elohim says that the Messiah is "the Way, and the Truth, and the Life" and that He is "the same yesterday, and today, and forever" (John 14:6; Hebrews 13:8). The same cannot be said of facts because they constantly change. I will give you an example. I am currently fifty-six years, one month, a few weeks, some days, some minutes and some seconds old. But in telling you that, the fact already has changed because I am now a few seconds older. So it goes on. Facts can change, but the truth remains constant. We would do well to understand that the Word of Elohim is the ultimate truth and never changes, ever! With it being the ultimate truth, it also can become very inconvenient because we like the convenient "truth."

> *Here is a great example. When my wife and I argue, I tend to clam up and be very quiet, but the Word says that if someone sins against me, I should go and make it right with that person (see Matthew 18:15). That is the truth, which is very inconvenient. Furthermore, Matthew 5:23-24 says that if I know someone is offended by me and is not coming to me, then I must go and make it right. More inconvenience! When we are angry or disappointed, then the truth does not always feel good and is definitely not easy to do.*

Step 3: Repent
One definition for *repent* that I prefer is to change your thinking. That is easier said than done, but we are commanded to do so in Romans 12:2:

> **"And do not be conformed to this world, but be transformed by the renewing of your mind, so that you prove what is that good and well-pleasing and perfect desire of Elohim."**

Notice carefully how we are commanded to "not be conformed to this world." In other words, we are not to follow worldly standards but to be transformed in our minds. Most people want to be changed without having to work at it; the magic must just happen without our efforts. The Word of Elohim clearly tells us a different story. Our thinking has to change in order for progress to be made. We have to come to repentance, and repentance means to change the way we think about things.

> *To illustrate the point, we take the story of "Dave," a married man who is having an affair with his secretary. This worries Dave, but not to the point of repentance. As the affair goes on, Dave realizes that his affair is wrong and*

The Power of Action

eventually decides to stop because he is convicted of his action. Dave has come to repentance because he changed the way that he thought about what he was doing.

Without repentance, there will be no change in our behavior and so we will never experience healing and restoration. Once again, thinking plays a critical role in our healing. True repentance only happens when we change our thinking and align it with the thinking of the Word.

Repent and change your mind.

The following passage of scripture fully illustrates this for us:

"But Elohim has revealed them to us through His Spirit. For the Spirit searches all matters, even the depths of Elohim. For who among men knows the thoughts of a man except the spirit of the man that is in him? So also, the thoughts of Elohim no one has known, except the Spirit of Elohim. And we have received, not the spirit of the world, but the Spirit that is from Elohim, in order to know what Elohim has favourably given us, which we also speak, not in words which man's wisdom teaches but which the Set-apart Spirit teaches, comparing spiritual matters with spiritual matters. But the natural man does not receive the matters of the Spirit of Elohim, for they are foolishness to him, and he is unable to know them, because they are spiritually discerned. But he who is spiritual discerns indeed all matters, but he himself is discerned by no one. For 'Who has known the mind

> *of יהוה? Who shall instruct Him?' But we have the mind of Messiah" (1 Corinthians 2:10-16).*

Again, when we are born again, we have the mind of the Messiah—or should have. But we allow it to be corrupted by our own thoughts and foolishness, then wonder why we do the things we do and don't do the things we should.

> *We are like computers. When we get a new computer, it boots up speedily, runs magnificently and operates the way it should. Then we start adding things onto the hard drive and it slows down a little. We plug into browsers we should not and pick up some viruses that slow the computer down even more. We are like the computers; we have polluted our systems with garbage and have picked up all sorts of viruses that corrupt us, slow us down and destroy our "hard drives" or brains. But there is great news here, for just as with any computer, we can download an anti-virus package that will clean up the viruses. We can reboot our hard drives if we follow the correct steps. But this cleanup will not happen on its own accord; we need to do it. We need to become aware that there is a problem with our hard drives, with our thinking, and we need to download the anti-virus package, the Spirit of Elohim, that will clean up our mess and restore the hard drive to its original condition.*

Confess.
Once you have decided to forgive someone, confess with your mouth this forgiveness and then, if possible, go and make it right with the one who offended you. You can do so with a phone call, an email, a letter or in person. If the person is no longer alive, then you have no further obligation to do anything because you

have done what was commanded of you. This is a hard thing to do, but bear in mind the Messiah hanging on the cross, beaten beyond physical recognition and bleeding. He lifts His eyes, the same eyes filled with love and compassion, to the Father who has forsaken Him because of our sin, and says, "Father, forgive them, for they do not know what they do" (Luke 23:34). How much more should you and I do the same?

> *"... You have received without paying, give without being paid" (Matthew 10:8).*

Step 4: Forgive
Forgiveness is a vital component in this process, for without forgiveness, true healing can never begin and never be completed. Forgiveness starts with a frame of mind, an attitude of our thinking, if you will. We often get hurt in life—some small thing someone said to us or some big thing someone did to us wounds us. No matter what it was, the tendency is for these things to take root in our lives and start killing us. Unforgiveness is a cancer: it will take hold of you, destroy you and kill you if you give it the chance.

> *I once knew a woman who stopped going to church for many years because another lady in the congregation said something nasty about her dress. The woman allowed the seed of unforgiveness to germinate in her life, and her decisions became based on unforgiveness.*

Something little and totally irrelevant can have such an influence on our lives that we perish from it, both spiritually and physically. Even the emotional effects of unforgiveness are quite alarming. Studies have shown that people who harbor unforgiveness can be emotionally and physically stressed, can de depressed and can even develop personality disorders if the situation is bad. We tend to see unforgiveness as a justified emotional response while it is, in fact, an active choice of the will that leads to our own death and destruction.

EMOTIONAL WHOLENESS

Remember that the goal of the enemy is "to steal, and to slaughter, and to destroy" (John 10:10).

Forgive no matter what.

A prime example of this unforgiveness was my grandmother. Her husband, my granddad, had gone off to World War II in 1939 as a volunteer and did not return until the end of the war in 1945. He was captured by the Germans in North Africa at the battle of Tobruk and had been a prisoner of war (POW) for many years. After he had died, and my gran lived with us, we were watching a show on television called The World at War, a fascinating documentary series about the war. This particular episode showed the life of prisoners in the POW camps. It was horrible. It must have been tough to deal with as a prisoner. I remember asking my gran if she knew that this was what her husband had been through, and her reply was rather brutal: "It was his fault; he signed up for this," she said. My gran was a very bitter woman who had resented her husband for decades; she had never forgiven him for leaving to go to war. Her bitterness and resentment showed and was made plain in her response.

Unforgiveness leads to anger and resentment and eventually to hate.

I have told this story before, but it bears repeating ... I am a middle child, the oldest son with an older sister and a younger brother. At age eight my parents split up, for about a year and a half. We

The Power of Action

were asked who we would like to live with. I chose my father, but my other two siblings went with my mother, so we all had to go live with my mom. This move started off a very long event in which I started resenting my mother. I was annoyed with her most of the time, and this feeling just grew and grew over the years. My folks got back together again, but my relationship with my mother was still terrible. I was constantly annoyed with her, and although we did not fight regularly, I hardly ever spoke to her unless I had to. This anger I had led to resentment, and the resentment eventually grew to a total hatred for the woman. At eighteen I was off to the military, and it was one of the best days of my life back then; I was going to be free from my mother and follow my desire to become a professional soldier. During basic training I received a call, which was strange because I had not told anyone where I was, and it was from my mother who had phoned the headquarters to find out where I was. I was not impressed, and I told my mother that if I wanted to speak to her, I would phone. I hardly ever did. This resentment stopped me from having a great relationship with my mother until I got radically saved in July of 1999. The following year, 2000, I had the opportunity to go to Canada for ten weeks where I attended the church of John and Carrol Arnott in Toronto. This in itself was a great miracle and blessing because it was where my healing truly started. I remember talking to friends after church and speaking about relationships. I asked Elohim why my relationship with my mother, in particular, and those with other women, were so toxic. Through the Spirit of Elohim, I was reminded of the situation when I was eight, and I was shown that I had harbored unforgiveness in my heart towards my mother all of those years. I

> *repented of my unforgiveness and asked Elohim to forgive me for my unforgiveness. When I returned home, I went to my mother to make it right with her. My mom and I have enjoyed a great relationship over the past twenty years because I was obedient to the prompting of the Spirit of Elohim and did what I was commanded to do. I was set free from the resentment and anger because of this repentance, and I point out to people with whom I share the story that in all of this my mother has not changed a bit—I did. I was set free and released, and I have benefited from the freedom. My mother has, too, but the crux of the matter is I was wrong, and I had made death choices up to the point of forgiveness. Life and death choices; blessing or curse. Choose wisely. Choose life.*

Have you ever been in a situation where you should have forgiven and did not? Or how about being in a situation where you needed to be forgiven, but weren't? How did you feel at the time? Were you better off not forgiving the person or not being forgiven? Think about this for a moment and ask yourself who needs to be forgiven, not who deserves it. You see, you and I will never deserve to be forgiven of our sins either. Forgiveness is about choice. You decide to forgive, or you decide not to forgive. If you cannot forgive, then it means that you have not received forgiveness. You cannot give what you don't have to give. The key is forgiveness, and the real drive of forgiveness is love. If you do not have love, then you will not be able to forgive.

Principle of Life: What you sow is what you reap.

> **"Do not be led astray: Elohim is not mocked, for whatever a man sows, that he shall also reap" (Galatians 6:7).**

> **"He who sows sparingly shall also reap sparingly" (2 Corinthians 9:6).**

Unforgiveness can be seen as you taking a drink from a vial of poison hoping the other person dies from it. It is a dangerous thing and should be treated as such. The Word of Elohim says, "Forgive us our debts, as we forgive our debtors" (Matthew 6:12) ... notice the condition here "as." What this verse is saying, and what we are praying, is that our debts are forgiven like we forgive the debts of others. So if we do not forgive others their debts, then ours won't be forgiven either. Matthew 6:14-15 carries on to say that *if* we forgive others their trespasses, then the heavenly Father will also forgive us of ours; but if we don't forgive them, then the Father will not forgive ours.

This is a powerful image here. Once again, the power of unforgiveness cannot be stressed enough. So, let us confirm a few things here:

1. Forgiveness is not an emotion; it is an active choice of the will.
2. Unforgiveness will cause you spiritual, emotional and physical harm.
3. You will be forgiven the same way that you forgive others.
4. Forgiveness requires repentance, a change of mind.

When we learn to forgive, we activate our Elohim-given right—and that is the will to choose. The Word of Elohim says:

> **"... I have set before you life and death, the blessing and the curse. Therefore you shall choose life, so that you live, both you and your seed" (Deuteronomy 30:19).**

Notice here that the choices are clear-cut; there is not an abundance of options ranging from life, to ninety percent of life, to eighty percent of life, etc., all the way down to death. There is life and there is death; there is blessing and there is curse. I love the fact that Elohim is a God of black and white; there is no middle road, there are no gray areas, there is just life and death. We need to start seeing our lives in this light. We need to start making choices based on life and death and blessing and curse. When we do so, we will begin to see radical changes in our lives; we will have clear vision and see things in the way Elohim intended for us to see them. Unforgiveness is a death choice and leads to the curse. When we forgive, we are making a life choice that leads to blessing.

> *There is a great testimony I once heard of a seventeen-year-old boy who was part of a church group. In order to get to the church, they had to go through a bar to get to the upper room. One time as they were walking through the bar, he noticed an elderly man sitting alone in the corner. The man was not engaging with the other patrons and was drinking on his own. The boy approached the church leader and told him that Elohim had told to go to the elderly gentleman and give him a specific message. The church leader was shocked at the content of the message but allowed the boy to deliver it. The young lad, full of courage, went up to the man and told him this: "Elohim says it is okay; I also killed My own Son." The gentleman broke down and through counseling it was revealed that the father had accidentally shot his son on a hunting trip and had vowed to drink himself into oblivion, which he had begun to do. Through this, the father was able to forgive himself and start the healing process in his own life.*

This story clearly illustrates the power of life and death choices. This man had chosen death over life; he had chosen curse over blessing; and it was in operation in his life. When we choose unforgiveness, even towards ourselves, we choose death and curse. We choose to die spiritually, emotionally and physically. We bring about a curse on ourselves that leads to death. I will go so far as to say that unforgiveness is a sin, and we know that "the wages of sin is death" (Romans 6:23). We need to choose forgiveness; we need to choose life and blessing. It is worthwhile to notice here that Yahweh can and will use other things and circumstances to reveal things to us that we might not be aware of.

We are commanded:

> *"... You have received without paying, give without being paid" (Matthew 10:8).*

This scripture talks about what we have received from above, without cost. So, since we have received forgiveness at no cost to ourselves, it is commanded that we give it away at no cost to others.

Principle of Life: We cannot give what we don't have.

This means that if we don't have something, we can never give it. I have counselled parents and children alike and asked them for an exorbitant amount of cash, knowing that they could never give it because they don't have it. When they respond that they cannot do it, I have asked them why. The response is always the same: "I don't have it to give." This realization that we cannot give what we do not have is a great starting point for moving forward. But, it is true for more than just money. If we don't have respect, how do we give it? If we don't have patience, how do we give it? If we don't have forgiveness, how do we give it? And if we don't have love, how do we give it?

Forgiveness starts with us first receiving it from above. After we accept forgiveness, we can then give it away to others. Receiving forgiveness is not a selective event; it is not reserved for those who deserve it. You and I are in that same category; we never deserved our forgiveness either, so how can we expect others to deserve it as well?

Forgiveness is not reserved for just those who deserve it.

Let's take a look at the story of the king in Matthew 18. The Messiah is telling the story to Peter, His disciple, who asked how many times he must forgive someone. The Messiah tells a story about a rich king who calls up his servants who owe him money so that he can get them to settle up their debts. The one servant owes the king millions of dollars, or as was said at that time, "ten thousand talents." Think about it for a moment. There was no possible way for this servant to have racked up so much debt, and there was even less chance that he could have ever repaid the loan. The king orders the servant to be sold, along with his wife and kids and everything else they possess, in order to recover some of the costs. The servant begs the king for mercy and asks for more time to repay the money. It was not possible for this servant to have even been able to make that kind of money to repay the loan. The king, having pity on the servant, decides to forgive him and cancels the loan completely. There is no more debt; the servant is free from it. One would think that the servant would be overjoyed at this news and celebrate his debt forgiveness, but instead he goes to another servant who owes him a few thousand dollars, or "a hundred denarii," and demands that the servant repay his debt. When the fellow servant could not repay him, the first servant has him thrown into prison until the debt is repaid. The king is told about it by other servants, and the king has the servant whom he forgave brought before him again. The king, livid and angry, rebukes the servant and has him thrown into jail and tortured until his debt is repaid.

The Messiah finishes the story by saying this: "So also My heavenly Father shall do to you if each of you, from his heart, does not forgive his brother his trespasses" (Matthew 18:35). This is quite a story, and it illustrates the point that since we have received without paying, so we should give without being paid (see Matthew 10:8).

Have you ever been in that position, where you received forgiveness? What did it make you feel like, knowing that it was something you should never have gotten? Have you ever been in a situation where you should have forgiven someone else but failed to do so? How did that make you feel? You see, it works both ways; it is a series of give and ... no, not take, it is give and receive. You have received without paying, so give without being paid, as the scripture says.

Forgiving another may take a while to do, as the father of all lies will try to tell you that the person does not deserve to be forgiven. That statement may sound good; it may be factual; but we are dealing with truth here, and our obedience to Elohim will be a blessing to us. Remember, the devil has one goal, and that is "to steal, and to slaughter, and to destroy" (John 10:10). There is nothing else that matters to the devil, so be wary of the lies. You may have to forgive this person daily. Do it anyways because the more you do it, the less it bothers you.

When you are obedient to Elohim, you release a blessing on yourself. You release "the substance of what is expected, the proof of what is not seen" (Hebrews 11:1). If you can contact the person, then I urge you to do so. I urge you to phone or email or send a letter.

Walk in Forgiveness
Choose to walk in forgiveness daily, as long as today is today. In Matthew 18:21-22 when Peter approaches Yeshua and asks Him how many times he has to forgive those who sin against him, he asks, "Up to seven times?" Yeshua answers and says it is not up to seven times, "but up to seventy times seven." Thus we are commanded here to forgive often and repeatedly. Remember, we will be forgiven our sins as we forgive those who sin against us (see Matthew 6:12; Colossians 3:13). We must forgive if we are to bring blessing to ourselves. When we choose unforgiveness, we choose death and curse upon ourselves. Today we have life and death choices before us, and we are encouraged to choose life. Unforgiveness and disobedience are death choices. It will require faith, obedience and courage to do the right thing.

> *"He who believes in the Son possesses everlasting life, but he who does not obey the Son shall not see life, but the wrath of Elohim remains on him" (John 3:36).*

Following is a brief guide you can use to follow the process to emotional wholeness. Take courage and follow the path to freedom.
Shalom.

QUICK GUIDE
A Step-by-Step Guide for the Healing Process

Stage	Step	Action Required
Reveal	Pray and Fast (Ask)	Go into a time of prayer and fasting and ask Almighty Elohim for a revelation of the things that require healing in your life. Write down the area/s that have been shown to you by the Spirit of Elohim so that you can work through them one by one.
Deal	Accept Responsibility	
Deal	Be Obedient	When the Spirit of Elohim reveals to you what needs to be done, then be obedient to the call. You will be required to act on the command so that the will and desire of Elohim can be fulfilled in your life.
Deal	Repent	Repent of your sins; ask and receive forgiveness.
Deal	Forgive	Speak forgiveness over the people whom you need to forgive. Where possible, personally talk to the individuals involved to ask them to forgive you. (This can be a text or an email.)
Heal	Walk in Forgiveness	Repeat this process as many times as you need to until you are whole.

www.ingramcontent.com/pod-product-compliance
Lightning Source LLC
Chambersburg PA
CBHW072003110526
44592CB00012B/1193